New e for English

5e

A2

Direction pédagogique
Mélanie HERMENT
Enseignante et formatrice
Académie de Paris

Coordination pédagogique
Pascaline GOUYETTE
Enseignante
Académie de Paris

AUTEURES

Anna GUILL
Enseignante et formatrice
Académie de Versailles

Laura CURSAT
Enseignante
Académie de Besançon

Mélanie HERMENT

Astrid BEFFARA
Enseignante
Académie de Créteil

Karine LETELLIER
Enseignante
Académie de Paris

Corinne LETANT
Enseignante
Académie de Paris

Pascaline GOUYETTE

Carine FAUVERT
Enseignante et formatrice
Académie de Montpellier

didier

Remerciements

Les auteurs et l'éditeur remercient chaleureusement les enfants qui ont contribué, par leurs témoignages, à donner au projet son identité culturelle : Sky et River D'Costa-Stephenson, Camry Tardy, Karlee Benot, Rhea Johri, Imogen Day, Alabama Howdle Fuller, Charlotte Pons, Melisa Campbell, Harriet Riddiough, Zoe Marsland, Pooja Pillai, Mai-Linh et Emile Grabiel, Imran Gardner, Josephine Seum Souk, Kayo Pouchous, Akash et Amrita Vukoti, Noe Vinchon-Noirel, Mohit, Karan et Yamini Rathore, Ruby Sprinkle.

Ils expriment également toute leur gratitude à Julie Spencer, de Notting Hill and Ealing High School, Elisabeth King, du Lycée Français de New York, et Myriam Aich, à Mumbai, pour leur aide inestimable dans la mise au point des chapitres et l'organisation des tournages et enregistrements avec leurs élèves et connaissances.

L'éditeur exprime toute sa reconnaissance à Annie Coghlan pour sa relecture attentive et exigeante et ses suggestions toujours pertinentes, qui ont grandement bénéficié à l'ensemble du projet.

Édition : Claudine Varin, Claire Laloue

Responsable éditoriale : Catherine Laurent

Conception maquette intérieure : Anne-Danielle Naname

Conception couverture : Nicolas Piroux

Mise en page : Anne-Danielle Naname, Adeline Calame, Dany Mourain

Illustrations : Sylvie Eder, Johanna Crainmark, John Royle, Kerry Hyndmann

Cartes et graphiques : Johanna Crainmark

Iconographie : Sophie Labrousse, Magali Girodet

Photogravure : Anne-Danielle Naname

 ISBN : 978-2-278-10512-0

Bienvenue en 5e !

Cette année, nous allons t'aider à **consolider tes connaissances en anglais**. Avec *E for English* 5e, tu vas pouvoir :

Poursuivre ta découverte du monde anglophone

Tu as sûrement beaucoup de questions.
Poudlard et Serpentard, ça existe pour de vrai dans les écoles britanniques ?
Le sport est-il aussi important pour les Américains que ce qu'on voit au cinéma ?
Que font les adolescents américains pendant leurs vacances ?
Et il y a encore plein d'autres pays où l'on parle anglais ! Tu vas en avoir un aperçu à travers les fêtes célébrées en Inde et en Irlande, et tu vas même pouvoir en organiser une dans ton collège !

Mener des projets motivants

Jouer à *Time's Up!*, écrire la suite d'une histoire, acheter un billet de cinéma et commander au restaurant, créer ta propre colonie de vacances et même... participer à un *escape game* !

Grâce à tous nos partenaires dans le monde, tu écouteras et liras un anglais authentique et tu participeras à des activités motivantes !

Gagner en autonomie

Nous t'offrons des pages qui te sont exclusivement destinées ! Des pages d'informations et d'activités ludiques en fin de chapitre mais aussi une bande dessinée passionnante, à lire en épisodes.
E for English te permettra également de réfléchir à la manière dont tu travailles en anglais, pour devenir de plus en plus autonome.

Écouter de l'anglais tous les jours

Pour finir, nous te lançons un défi : écouter quelques minutes d'anglais tous les jours grâce aux nombreux audios et vidéos que nous te proposons. Dans ton *workbook*, tu peux même gagner des étoiles. Tu progresseras à l'oral à vitesse grand V !

Nous te souhaitons une année d'anglais joyeuse et enrichissante !

Les auteures

River

Sky

River et Sky,
collégiens à Londres

Chapitre 1

Rhea & Melissa

Imogen

Charlotte

Les élèves
de NHEHS,
à Londres

Chapitre 3

Alabama & Zane

Ils te font découvrir le monde anglophone

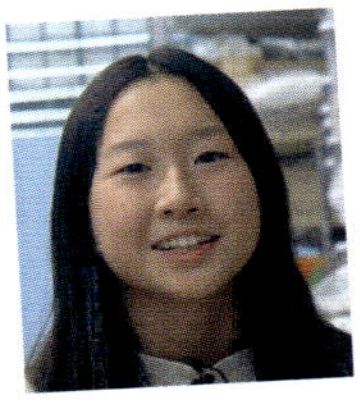

Josephine

Kayo

Lucia

Imran

Eddie

Les élèves du Lycée
Français de New York

Chapitre 6

Camry

Camry, étudiante
sportive du Texas

Chapitre 2

Ruby

Ruby, lycéenne
en Floride

Chapitre 8

... Et pour parler
des fêtes en Inde :
Noe, Amrita et Akash

Chapitre 7

Noe

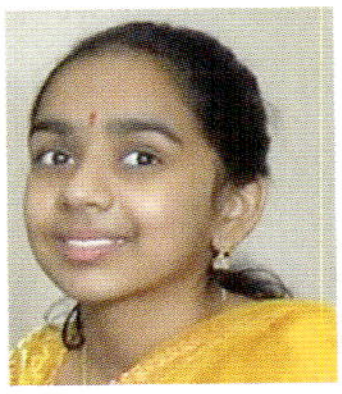

Amrita

Akash

1 chapitre ludique
pour bien démarrer l'année

Révisions

PROJECT 1

Who's who?

p. 12

Découvertes culturelles
- Les personnages célèbres de la fiction britannique
- Rencontre avec des collégiens britanniques

LESSON 1 p. 14

Vocabulaire	La description physique Les vêtements et accessoires
Grammaire	*BE* et *HAVE* au Présent simple Questions fermées / réponses courtes L'adjectif qualificatif

- Écouter la description de personnages et les identifier
- Jouer à faire deviner des personnages

MINI TASK!
Jouer au « Who's who? »

LESSON 2 p. 16

Vocabulaire	La personnalité Les centres d'intérêts
Grammaire	Les déterminants possessifs Le Présent simple
Prononciation	L'accent de mot L'accent de phrase

- Comprendre de jeunes britanniques qui décrivent leur personnalité
- Répondre à un test de personnalité fondé sur les personnages des *Mr. Men & Little Misses*

MINI TASK!
Sur le modèle des *Mr. Men & Little Misses*, créer son propre personnage

FINAL TASK! p. 18

Jouer à Time's up!

NEED HELP? S'entraîner à bien prononcer

Dans ce premier chapitre, révise les notions de l'année de 6e en jouant avec tes camarades !

ACTIVITÉ NUMÉRIQUE

Pour la classe

Guess the character!

Dans les chapitres qui suivent, consolide tes connaissances tout en poursuivant les apprentissages et les découvertes !

7 projets
Pour s'investir et progresser en 5^{e}

PROJECT 2

Cheer for your team!

p. 28

Découvertes culturelles
- L'importance du sport aux États-Unis, à l'école et dans la société
- Les rencontres sportives lors de la fête de Thanksgiving

LESSON 1 p. 30

Vocabulaire	Le sport à l'école Les sentiments et opinions
Grammaire	Les déterminants *the/a(n)* L'expression de la fréquence
Prononciation	L'accentuation des noms composés

- Comprendre une page de yearbook sur *Friday Night Lights*
- Écouter le témoignage d'une jeune spectatrice

MINI TASK!
Compléter une page de yearbook

LESSON 2 p. 32

Vocabulaire	Les traditions de Thanksgiving Les événements sportifs
Grammaire	Le Présent *BE* + V-*ing*
Prononciation	La prononciation des verbes en *-ing*

- Comprendre une vidéo sur une rencontre sportive lors de Thanksgiving
- Découvrir les rituels liés à cette fête

MINI TASK!
Jeu de mime : faire deviner un personnage, un lieu, une action

FINAL TASK! p. 34

Créer une page de yearbook

NEED HELP? Commenter des images

ACTIVITÉ NUMÉRIQUE
Pour la classe
Sports Memory

READING CORNER p. 42
FENCE episode 1

PROJECT 3

Your house at school

p. 44

Découvertes culturelles
- Les « maisons » dans un établissement scolaire britannique
- Les biographies de femmes célèbres dont ces maisons portent le nom

LESSON 1 p. 46

Vocabulaire	L'école
Grammaire	Les noms composés *There is / There are*

- Comprendre des témoignages sur le système des maisons dans une école britannique
- Décrire le fonctionnement de ce système

MINI TASK!
Présenter sa candidature aux élections des capitaines de maisons

LESSON 2 p. 48

Vocabulaire	Les éléments d'une biographie
Grammaire	Le Prétérit simple
Prononciation	La terminaison *-ed* du Prétérit

- Lire un message publié sur Instagram par des *house captains*
- Comprendre les biographies de personnalités
- Écrire un tweet pour expliquer un choix

MINI TASK!
Choisir un nom pour une nouvelle maison

FINAL TASK! p. 50

Créer une maison pour son école

NEED HELP? Se documenter en vue d'une présentation

ACTIVITÉ NUMÉRIQUE
Pour la classe
Snakes & ladders

READING CORNER p. 58
FENCE episode 2

7 projets
Pour s'investir et progresser en 5e

PROJECT 5

Dinner and a movie

p. 86

Découvertes culturelles
- Le *dine-in theatre* : un cinéma typiquement américain !
- La nourriture américaine

LESSON 1 p. 88

Vocabulaire	Au cinéma
Grammaire	*want to / would like to* **Révisions :** Le pronom relatif *who*
Prononciation	Les lettres muettes : le « L » de *would* L'accentuation des chiffres

- Découvrir des affiches de films
- Comprendre de jeunes Américains qui choisissent un film et achètent leurs billets
- Consulter un programme de cinéma en ligne et faire son choix

MINI TASK!
Choisir un film et réserver une place sur un site de cinéma

LESSON 2 p. 90

Vocabulaire	Au restaurant
Grammaire	Les déterminants *a(n)*, ∅ **Révisions :** Les noms composés

- Comprendre un menu de restaurant
- Comprendre la commande passée par des clients à un serveur

MINI TASK!
Jeu de rôles : passer commande au restaurant

FINAL TASK! p. 92

Organiser une soirée cinéma et composer son menu

NEED HELP? Poser des questions et y répondre

ACTIVITÉ NUMÉRIQUE
Pour la classe
Order your food!

READING CORNER p. 100

FENCE episode 5

PROJECT 6

Take a Super Tour of New York City

p. 102

Découvertes culturelles
- La ville de New York en compagnie des élèves du Lycée Français et de... Spider-Man !

LESSON 1 p. 104

Vocabulaire	La ville (1)
Grammaire	Le superlatif de supériorité
Prononciation	Les sons /a:/, /ei/, /æ/

- Découvrir le personnage de Spider-Man à travers une planche de BD et un court article
- Identifier quelques lieux et monuments emblématiques de New York

MINI TASK!
Décrire et faire deviner un lieu ou un monument new yorkais

LESSON 2 p. 106

Vocabulaire	La ville (2) Donner ses impressions
Grammaire	Le comparatif de supériorité

- Découvrir la vie new yorkaise à travers les témoignages de jeunes lycéens

MINI TASK!
Jouer à *This or that?*

FINAL TASK! p. 108

Participer à une interview en tant qu'élève du Lycée Français de New York

NEED HELP? Donner son opinion et justifier ses choix

ACTIVITÉ NUMÉRIQUE
Pour la classe
Find the monument!

READING CORNER p. 116

FENCE episode 6

En fin de manuel

A little extra to Celebrate Saint Patrick's Day!

Grammar Essentials

Dans ton workbook

Pour chaque chapitre

Des supports motivants prêts à l'emploi pour les activités de classe

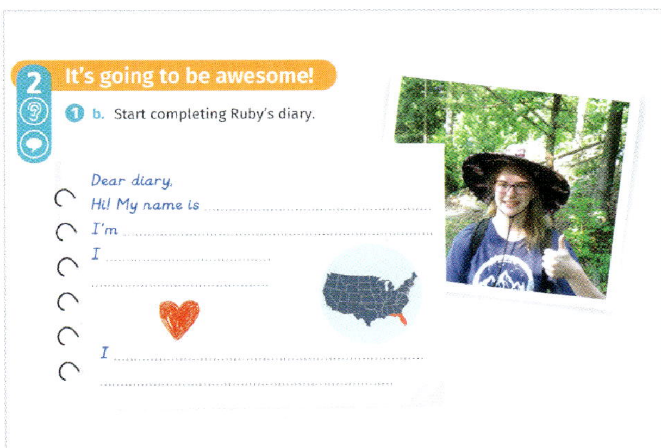

Des fiches « Mémo grammaire » à compléter et à coller dans ton cahier

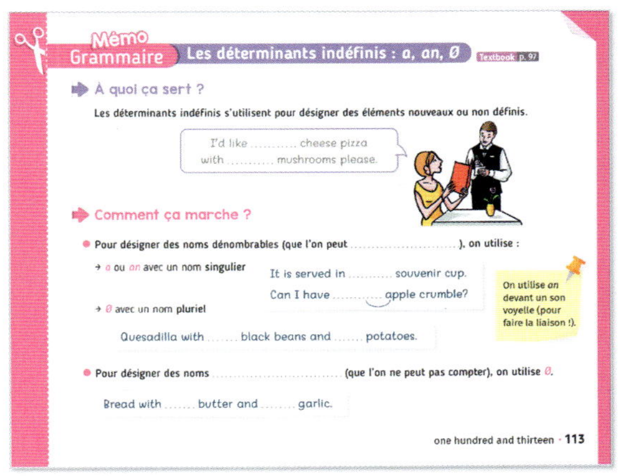

Des exercices de vocabulaire et de grammaire pour t'entraîner à la maison

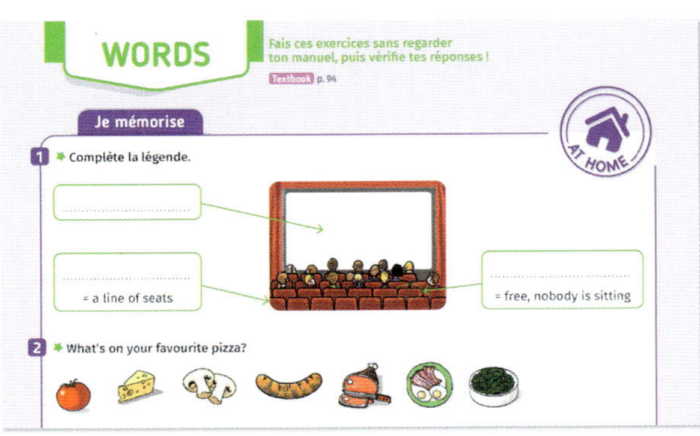

Des enregistrements courts et amusants pour progresser en compréhension de l'oral

AT HOME

PROJECT

1

Who's who?

Dans ce chapitre, tu vas :

- Rencontrer des Britanniques, réels ou fictifs, célèbres ou pas !
- Apprendre à présenter quelqu'un, à poser des questions… et à jouer en anglais ! 😊

Vocabulaire

- La description physique, les vêtements et accessoires
- La personnalité et les centres d'intérêt

Grammaire

- Le Présent simple : *BE, HAVE*, autres verbes
- L'adjectif qualificatif
- Les déterminants possessifs

JEU NUMÉRIQUE

Guess the character!

Play games with famous British characters and learn more about yourself!

CURIOUS
FUN
RIOUS
HELPFU

LESSON 1

Let's play!

Play with famous British characters

1

Enola Holmes

2

Sherlock Holmes

3

Cho Chang
in *Harry Potter*

4

Doctor Watson in
Sherlock Holmes

5

John Luther
in *Luther*

6

Mary Poppins

7

Albus Dumbledore

8

Matilda

9

M
in *James Bond*

10

Mr Bean

11

Tinker Bell
in *Peter Pan*

12

Harry Potter

13

Charlie Bucket
in *Charlie and the Chocolate Factory*

14

Eve Moneypenny
in *James Bond*

15

James Bond

16

Alice in
Alice in Wonderland

GAME TIME!

GAME 1 – Spot the characters

1. **Listen and spot the characters on p. 14.**
   Audio 22nefe5101

2. **Your turn!**
   Play with a classmate.
   Need Help? See Words p. 20.

Time to write First, practise building sentences. WB p. 4
Now write a character profile. Can your classmate find who it is?

GAME 2 – Who's who?

1. **Listen and play along in your workbook.** Audio 22nefe5102 WB p. 5

2. **Your turn! Play with your class.**

MINI TASK!

Play *Who's who?* with your classmate.

IN PAIRS

Get ready to ask or answer questions. WB p. 5

Is it a woman?

Yes, it is!

Does she have a headband?

Yes, she does!

Dans cette leçon, tu as appris :

Vocabulaire » p. 20
- La description physique
- Les vêtements et accessoires

Grammaire » p. 22-23
- *BE* et *HAVE* au Présent simple
- L'adjectif qualificatif

LESSON 2

Your personality!

1 Happy? Sociable? Funny?

Sky

River

1. **Brainstorming!** Start a class wordcloud with all the words you know to describe someone's personality.

   sociable happy **funny**

2. **Watch River and Sky talking about themselves.** Video 22nefe5103
   a. Complete their profiles in your workbook. WB
   b. Spot the Mr. Men or Little Miss character that best matches their personalities.

Mr... / Little Miss...

3. **Learn more words in your workbook.** WB p. 6
   Then add them to the class wordcloud.

2 Quiz time!

1. **How about you? Take the Quiz!** WB p. 7

Which "Little Miss" or "Mr. Men" character are you?

1
Pick a colour:
☐ green △ yellow ◯ pink ☆ navy

2
It's snowing outside and school is canceled. What do you decide to do?
☐ sleep the whole day
△ watch TV
◯ hang out with friends
☆ play in the snow

3

6
Imagine you have £1,000.
How do you want to spend it?
☐ food ◯ make-up
△ clothes ☆ electronics

7
Pick a superpower:
☐ strength ◯ flight
△ invisibility ☆ telepathy

8
What's your favourite season?

Adapted from Buzzfeed.com

2 Read the characters' portraits in your workbook. WB p. 8

Little Miss Shy

Congratulations, you got Little Miss Shy! Little Miss Shy is bashful, modest, and timid. Little Miss Shy is (as her name suggests) painfully shy, blushing like a tomato when she's nervous. However, remember that quiet people sometimes have the loudest minds!

Little Miss Helpful

Congratulations, you got Little Miss Helpful! Little Miss Helpful is caring, kind, and supportive. Little Miss Helpful loves to help out. She'll help you tie your shoelaces or even clean your house. She might even make your dinner and wash it up afterwards! Little Miss Helpful is an extremely positive person!

Mr Cool

Congratulations, you got Mister Cool. Mister Cool is chilled-out, kind and mellow. Who doesn't want to be friends with Mr Cool? He's the best person to hang out with because there's never a dull moment.

Little Miss Fun

Congratulations, you got Little Miss Fun. Little Miss Fun is entertaining, lively, and a party animal! You and Little Miss Fun love to dance and you two are always the centre of attention.

3 **Do you agree with the test results?**
Is there another character or personality type that describes you better?

MINI TASK!

Create your own Mr. Men or Little Miss character.

WB p. 8

1. **Think about your character's identity. You can base it on:**

   yourself | a celebrity | your imagination 😊

2. **Think about your character's...**

   name | looks | personality | tastes

3. **Take two separate sheets:**

draw your character

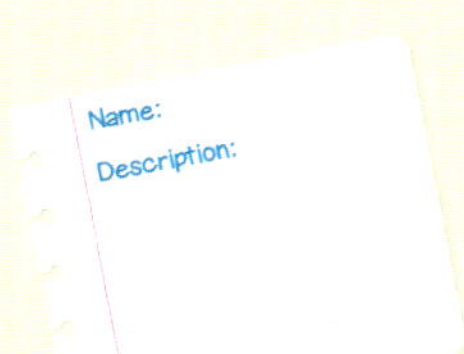

describe your character

4. **Can your classmates match your drawing with the description?**

Dans cette leçon, tu as appris :

Vocabulaire p. 20
- La personnalité
- Les centres d'intérêts

Grammaire p. 24-25
- Le Présent simple
- Les déterminants possessifs

FINAL TASK!

PLAY IN GROUPS OF FOUR

Let's play Time's up!

1 Choose your level

Divide your group into 2 teams of 2 pupils

LEVEL 1 **Play with the 16 characters from p. 14.** WB p. 121

LEVEL 2 **Play with your own cards.**

- Create 4 new cards each with famous British people:

sportspersons | singers | politicians | actors | ...

- Then mix the 16 cards.

- Revois les phrases affirmatives avec *BE* et *HAVE*.
- Écoute à nouveau le jeu. Audio efe5002
- Pense à utiliser le lexique p. 20 en écoutant les mots.

2 Play the level 1 or level 2 game.

There are 3 rounds.
Collect as many cards as possible! 1 card = 1 point

Round 1

- Pick a card.
- Tell your team-mate what you know about the character.
- If he/she guesses who it is, your team keeps the card!
- Then the other team tries to win a card too.

Round 1 ends when all the cards have been won. What is your score?

Round 2

- Pick a card and say only one word to describe your character.
- Your team-mate can only give one answer too!

Round 3

Pick a card and this time, mime it to your team-mate! If he/she guesses it right, you keep the card.

END

Count your points!!

NEED HELP? Follow the guide!

NEED HELP?

Du mot à la phrase, entraîne-toi à bien prononcer !

1 Accentue les bonnes syllabes

Audio 22nefe5104

Écoute ces mots et entraîne-toi à les prononcer :

woman | **car**ries | um**brel**la | **glas**ses | **ma**gic

Pour accentuer la syllabe d'un mot, fais monter le ton de ta voix et insiste légèrement sur cette syllabe :

*um**brel**la*

2 Fais les liaisons

Écoute maintenant ces mots dans des phrases. Entraîne-toi à les prononcer en respectant les liaisons indiquées (et toujours l'accent de mot !) :

It's a woman. (sə)

She carries a small umbrella. (zə) (lə)

He has a magic wand. (zə)

On fait la liaison quand le mot qui suit commence par un son voyelle.

3 Accentue les mots importants

Pour faire deviner ton personnage, tu peux insister davantage sur les mots qui permettent vraiment de l'identifier ou de le différencier d'un autre.

Doctor Watson

He has a **black** hat.

He has a **grey** hat.

Albus Dumbledore

4 Répétition générale !

Écoute et entraîne-toi à bien prononcer :

1. a small um**brel**la
2. She **car**ries a small um**brel**la.
3. She has a black hat.
4. She has a black hat // and she **car**ries a small um**brel**la.

- Entraîne-toi à passer du mot à la phrase.
- Fais bien les **liaisons** ◡ et les **pauses** // nécessaires.

Te voilà fin prêt(e) pour la FINAL TASK !

WORDS

Apprends ces mots avec leur prononciation !

Clothes and accessories

Audio 22nefe5105

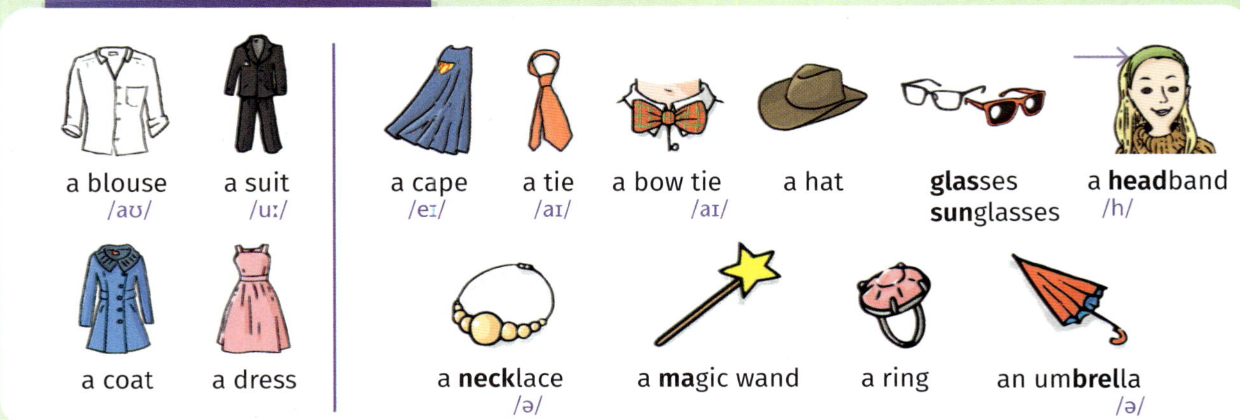

- a blouse /aʊ/
- a suit /uː/
- a coat
- a dress
- a cape /eɪ/
- a tie /aɪ/
- a bow tie /aɪ/
- a hat
- **glas**ses, **sun**glasses
- a **head**band /h/
- a **neck**lace /ə/
- a **ma**gic wand
- a ring
- an um**brel**la /ə/

Physical appearance

Audio 22nefe5106

- eyes /aɪ/
- ears /ɪə/
- mous**tache**
- nose
- mouth
- beard /ɪə/

hair /ɛə/

- short ≠ long
- straight ≠ curly /eɪ/
- a bun
- a ponytail
- blond, fair • brown • dark, black
- red
- grey
- young ≠ old
- slim ≠ fat
- tall ≠ small
- strong = **mus**cular

Personality

Audio 22nefe5107

- **so**ciable = outgoing
- **help**ful
- shy, **ti**mid
- kind = nice /aɪ/ /aɪ/
- **ge**nerous ≠ **sel**fish /dʒɛ/
- **ea**sygoing = cool
- **ner**vous /ɜː/
- brave = cou**ra**geous /eɪ/ /kəˈreɪdʒəs/
- **cle**ver = smart
- **fun**ny
- fun ≠ **bo**ring

Interests

Audio 22nefe5108

- dance
- hang out with friends
- help **peo**ple
- act
- sing
- solve **puz**zles

Vêtements et accessoires

1 ✱✱ **Little Miss Splendid joue aux devinettes avec toi !** Sauras-tu retrouver les vêtements ou accessoires qu'elle décrit ?

L'apparence physique

2 ✱✱ **Sherlock Holmes a établi le portrait robot d'un voleur de bijoux. Écoute sa description et identifie-le parmi ces trois suspects.**

Audio 22nefe5109

3 ✱✱✱ **Crée un nouveau compagnon d'aventures pour un des personnages p. 14.**
Dessine-le et rédige un texte pour le décrire.

La personnalité

4 **a.** ✱ **Choisis quatre adjectifs de la liste *Personality* que tu considères comme des qualités.**

b. Associe chacun de ces adjectifs à une personne que tu connais. Fais une phrase pour en parler.

Exemple :

My grandmother is kind.

5 ✱✱ **Utilise les lettres de ton prénom pour écrire un poème sur toi.**

6 ✱✱ **Ton camarade cherche ses mots. Aide-le à finir ses phrases en proposant un mot précis.**

Exemple : Ronnie is not reserved, he is … .
→ …, he is outgoing.

1. Draco Malfoy is not generous at all, he is …
2. This book is not fun, it is…
3. She seems worried and afraid. She looks …
4. My neighbours like to help. They are …
5. My little sister is not stupid, she is …

7 ✱✱✱ Work in teams. **Jouez au « petit Bac » : pour chaque catégorie, trouvez au moins un mot commençant par la lettre choisie.** Quelle équipe trouvera le plus de mots en 2 minutes ?

Exemple : Letter **g**

Colour	grey
Clothes/accessories	…
Physical description	…
Personality	generous
Character	…
Action / Interests	…

8 Prononciation

Audio 22nefe5110

a. Écoute et répète ces mots en faisant bien attention à l'accentuation.

headband – **ma**gic – **mus**cular – **out**going – **peo**ple – perso**na**lity – **ge**nerous – **cle**ver – **neck**lace

b. Écoute et entraîne-toi à prononcer ces phrases.

1. Mary Poppins has a beautiful necklace.
2. Harry Potter is courageous.
3. Little Miss Shy often gets nervous.
4. Little Miss Helpful is clever and supportive.

L'accent de mot

- En anglais, les mots de deux syllabes ou plus comportent toujours une **syllabe accentuée**.
- Les autres syllabes sont non accentuées.
- Quand une voyelle se trouve dans une syllabe non accentuée, elle est souvent prononcée /ə/ : on l'entend à peine.

nervous (ə) **ge**nerous (ə ə) cou**ra**geous (ə ə)

Poursuis l'entraînement WB p. 9

BE et *HAVE* au Présent simple

➡ Pour se présenter ou présenter quelqu'un, on peut avoir besoin du verbe *BE*.

Forme affirmative
I **am**
you **are**
he / she / it **is**
we **are**
you **are**
they **are**

This is a young lady. She is British. She is 21 years old.

Question time

Is he young? Yes he **is**.
No, he **is**n't.
auxiliaire *BE*

➡ Pour dire ce que l'on possède, on peut utiliser le verbe *HAVE*.

Forme affirmative
I **have**
you **have**
he / she / it **has**
we **have**
you **have**
they **have**

He has glasses.

Question time

Does she have long hair? Yes, she **does**.
No, she **does**n't.
have : base verbale
Does : auxiliaire du Présent simple **DO / DOES**

Souviens-toi 🙂
On utilise :
He pour un garçon / homme
She pour une fille / femme
It pour une chose ou un animal non familier
They pour plusieurs personnes ou choses.

1 ★ **Complète ces phrases à l'aide de *BE* conjugué.**
Ajoute aussi le pronom personnel sujet lorsqu'il manque !

1. It ... pink. 2. ... ... clever! 3. ... ... funny! 4. ... ... good friends!

2 ★★ **Observe les personnages p. 14 et complète les phrases avec *HAVE* conjugué.**

1. Mr Bean ... a brown teddy bear.
2. Sherlock Holmes and Mary Poppins ... hats.
3. Eve Moneypenny ... an umbrella.
4. Matilda and Harry Potter ... brown hair.
5. Alice ... a bun.

Utilise la forme négative si besoin !

3 ★★ **Connais-tu les personnages de *His Dark Materials* ? →**
Complète leur présentation à l'aide de *BE* ou *HAVE* conjugués.

1. Lyra ... a young girl. She ... a magic object to detect liars*.
2. Lord Asriel ... Lyra's father. He ... tall and powerful. He ... fierce, dark eyes.
3. Armoured bears ... very strong and intelligent. They ... a king: Lorek.

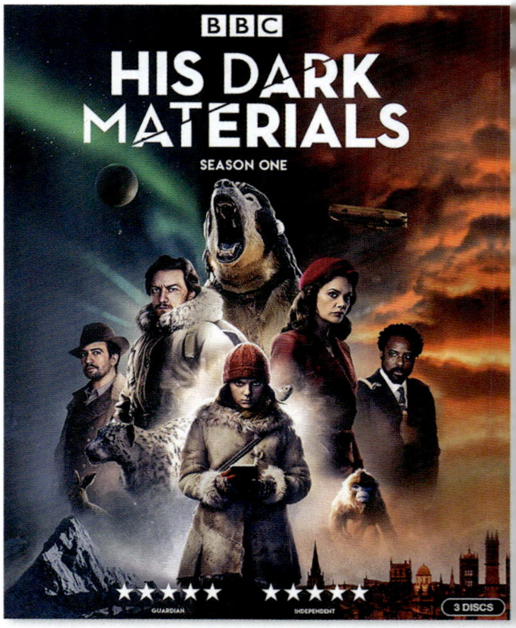

* liars : *menteurs*

LESSON 1

L'adjectif qualificatif

Pour apporter des précisions au nom, on peut utiliser des adjectifs qualificatifs.

Alice has big brown eyes.
adj. adj. nom

• Tu veux utiliser plusieurs adjectifs ? Attention à l'ordre :

A wonderful old lady.

Opinion + Taille + Age + Forme + Couleur + Origine + Matière + Nom

A large wooden box.

Pour te souvenir de cet ordre 🙂 Retiens **OTAFCOM**

- L'adjectif qualificatif est **invariable**.
- Lorsqu'il est épithète, on le place **avant** le nom qu'il qualifie.

4 ★ **Observe les personnages de la p. 14. Complète les descriptions en utilisant ces adjectifs, et trouve de qui il s'agit !**

magic | brown | black | curly | round | big | green

1. She has short ... dark hair. → It's ...
2. She has a ... dress and a ... bun. → It's ...
3. He has a ... teddy bear and ... hair. → It's ...
4. He has ... glasses and a ... wand. → It's ...

5 ★★ IN PAIRS **a. Choisis l'un de ces personnages de *Charlie et la Chocolaterie* et écris quelques phrases pour le décrire.**
Tu peux utiliser : *big / small / short / tall / hooked / grey / black ...*

b. Lis ta description à un(e) camarade. A-t-il/elle identifié ton personnage?

Grandpa Joe — Charlie Bucket — Willy Wonka

6 ★★ **Tu as identifié l'espion ennemi ! Afin de rendre ta description plus précise, ajoute un ou deux adjectifs pour qualifier chaque nom.**

This is a spy. He has scary eyes and short hair. He has a shirt and a bow tie.

This is a dangerous spy! He ...

Tu peux utiliser les adjectifs p. 20. Attention à l'ordre des adjectifs lorsqu'il y en a plusieurs !

7 ★★★ **Le prochain *James Bond* est en préparation ! Imagine son nouvel ennemi et décris-le au directeur de casting.**

Mets 2 adjectifs par élément... ou plus si tu peux !

CHARACTER LIST
The villain

MAN AGED 30-35

1. Eyes/hair/face
   This villain is very scary.
   He has ...
2. Clothes
   He has...
3. Pet
   He has a ...
4. Car
   He has a ...

Poursuis l'entraînement WB p. 11

Les déterminants possessifs

➡ Pour exprimer un lien entre deux éléments (parenté, appartenance...), on peut utiliser des déterminants possessifs.

my
your
his / her / its
our
your
their

Little Miss Shy is, as her name suggests, very shy.

Mr. Lazy's bed is his favourite place.

- Ces déterminants s'accordent avec le possesseur (ou « référent »).

Souviens-toi 🙂
His pour un référent masculin
Her pour un référent féminin
Its quand le référent est une chose ou un animal non familier

1 ✱ **Du chocolat est tombé sur le début de ce récit. Peux-tu retrouver les déterminants possessifs manquants ?**

"… name is Willy. Willy Wonka.
Open … ears and listen to … story!
I have a big factory.
Five children can visit it if they
have … golden tickets.
Here are two of … guests:
Charlie is with … grandpa and Violet
with … mother. Join us on … tour!!!

2 ✱✱ **Que peuvent bien dire ces personnages ? Complète à l'aide de déterminants possessifs.**

1. **Mary Poppins:** "I never forget ... umbrella when I go out."
2. **Cho Chang and Harry Potter**: "We go to the same school. ... name is Hogwarts. The headmaster of ... school is Albus Dumbledore."
3. **Mr Bean:** "I have a teddy bear. ... name is Teddy."
4. **Charlie Bucket:** "Do you know Willy Wonka? ... factory makes tons of chocolate!"
5. **Matilda's teacher:** "Matilda is intelligent and kind but ... parents are not!"

3 ✱✱ **Raconte l'histoire de Matilda en remplaçant les mots soulignés par des déterminants possessifs.**

1. Matilda and Michael are siblings. Michael and Matilda's father, Mr Wormwood, is a dishonest man.
2. Mr Wormwood sells cars. Mr Wormwood's cars are very expensive.
3. Matilda has friends. Matilda's best friend is Miss Honey.
4. Miss Honey is Matilda's teacher.

Matilda

4 ✱✱ **Complète ce témoignage d'un personnage connu avec les bons déterminants possessifs (ils peuvent être utilisés plusieurs fois).**

... friends are Hermione and Ron.
Ron is very funny, and ... brothers
are prefects in the school.
Hermione is very hardworking.
She does ... homework all the time.
In fact, we do ... homework together.
What about you?
Who are ... friends?

LESSON 2

Le Présent simple

➡ Lorsqu'on veut donner une information, on utilise le Présent simple.

- **Forme affirmative**

I phone my friends every day.

She loves to help out.

I like
you like
he / she / it likes
we like
you like
they like

- On utilise simplement la base verbale.
- À la 3e personne du singulier, on ajoute un –s à la base verbale.

- **Forme négative**

On fait appel à l'auxiliaire *DO / DOES*.

I don't like to dance.
= do not

She doesn't speak much.
= does not

C'est *DO* qui prend :
- la marque de la négation *not*
- le -s à la 3e personne du singulier

Question time

Which character do you prefer?
What does he like?
auxiliaire *DO / DOES* — base verbale

5 ✱✱ **Utilise des mots de chaque colonne pour dire ce qui est vrai pour toi ou tes proches.**

N'oublie pas de conjuguer les verbes !

I my best friend my mum / dad my cousins	like not like love hate	to dance to eat good food to sleep to help others to read mangas

6 ✱✱ **a.** ***Bond... James Bond***
James Bond est un espion mais il a une vie privée comme tout le monde !

Complète en conjuguant les verbes au Présent simple.

James Bond ... (*eat*) breakfast just like anyone else. I ... (*be*) sure he ... (*drink*) Earl Grey in the morning and ... (*love*) scrambled eggs. As he ... (*be*) a spy, he ... (*not/ have*) a lot of time so I imagine he ... (*eat*) sandwiches for lunch. But when he ... (*have*) the time, I ... (*be*) certain he ... (*enjoy*) a gourmet dinner in a fancy restaurant.

✱✱✱ **b. À ton tour, choisis un héros de fiction et imagine son quotidien.**

7 ✱✱ **Conjugue les verbes au Présent simple pour retrouver les citations des livres de Roald Dahl.**

1. 'Poor Earthworm,' the Ladybird said, [...] 'He ... (*love*) to make everything into a disaster. He ... (*hate*) to be happy.' **James and the Giant Peach**
2. "My darling," she said at last, "are you sure you ... (*not/mind*) being a mouse for the rest of your life?"
"I ... (*not/mind*) at all," I said.
"It ... (*not/matter*) who you are or what you ... (*look*) like, so long as somebody ... (*love*) you." **The Witches**
3. "I ... (be) right and you... (*be*) wrong, I ... (*be*) big and you ... (*be*) small, and there ... (*be*) nothing you can do about it." **Matilda**

8 Prononciation Audio 22nefe5111

a. Écoute cette phrase et entraîne-toi à la prononcer.

Mr **Cool** has **tons** of **friends**. That's because he's **very sociable**!

b. Écoute un dialogue et entraîne-toi à le prononcer.

L'accent de phrase
Dans une phrase en anglais, seuls les mots les plus importants sont accentués. Ce sont ceux que l'on entend le mieux !

Poursuis l'entraînement
WB p. 12

Choose your activities!

Early finishers

Guess who I am!

- I was born on July 31, 1965.
- I was born in Bristol, England.
- My real name is Joanne, but people know me by my two initials.
- I write books for children.
- My saga includes 7 books and 8 films.

Answer: J.K. Rowling

Did you know about... Holmes and Holmes ?!

Sir Arthur Conan Doyle, a British writer and physician, created Sherlock Holmes in 1887. Doyle was also an amateur detective: he solved a couple of real mysteries!

Holmes is the most portrayed literary human character in film & TV, with more than 250 productions*!

* Guinness World Records

→ **Riddle: Help Sherlock Holmes find the name of the killer!**
Use this secret message to find out the 4 letters of his name.

The killer's name is JOHN (January-October-March-June)

The eyes quiz

1 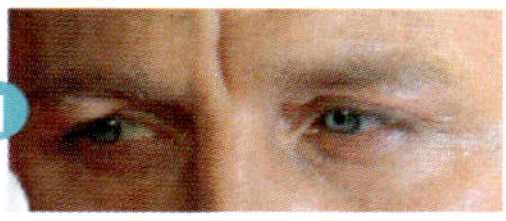
2 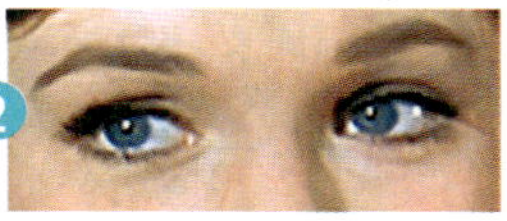
3 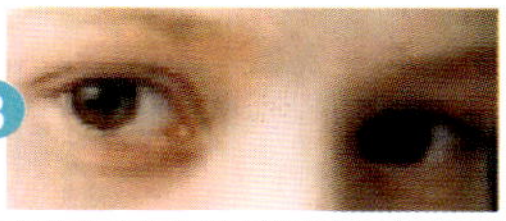
4 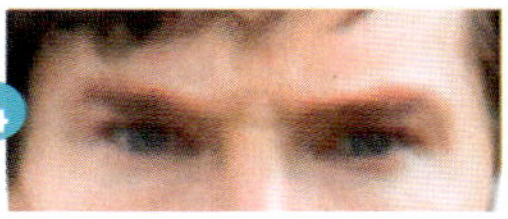

CLUES

ⓐ He's very clever and likes to solve puzzles. The answer is elementary, my dear reader!

ⓑ He's sophisticated and brave. He likes gadgets and fights villains.

ⓒ She likes to look after children. She is strict but kind.

ⓓ She's very polite but also very curious. She loves animals... especially white rabbits!

→ **Whose eyes are these?**
Use the clues and find the characters!

1b James Bond – **2c** Mary Poppins – **3d** Alice in Wonderland – **4a** Sherlock Holmes

The Enola Holmes Mysteries (2006-2010) is a series of 6 detective novels by American author Nancy Springer. Enola Holmes is the 14-year-old sister of Sherlock Holmes. However, she did not exist in Conan Doyle's novels!
The *Enola Holmes* novels have been adapted as graphic novels and as a movie.

Why not read the graphic novels and watch the movie?

This is the film based on the first book.

→ **Anagram: Use the letters in the name Enola to find out how she feels!**

Alone

Let's riddle!

Tom Marvolo Riddle

→ **What is the anagram of Tom Marvolo Riddle in *Harry Potter*?**

The name „Tom Marvolo Riddle", first mentioned in *Harry Potter and the Chamber of Secrets*, is rearranged to spell „I am Lord Voldemort".

PROJECT

2

Cheer for your team!

Dans ce chapitre, tu vas :

- Découvrir l'importance et l'énorme popularité du sport dans la culture américaine
- Créer une page de *yearbook* sur une manifestation sportive américaine

Vocabulaire

- Le sport
- La fête de Thanksgiving

Grammaire

- Les déterminants : *a(n)* / *the*
- L'expression de la fréquence
- Le Présent *BE* + V-*ing*

JEU NUMÉRIQUE
Sports Memory

Discover sports in American life and join the fun!

Fans celebrate during a college football game (Appalachian State, USA)

LESSON 1

Get into game spirit!

Friday night lights - What is your role?

FRIDAY NIGHT *lights*

CHEERLEADER

The main role of a cheerleader is to get the whole school excited about the game during the week before the event. And then on Friday, we cheer on our team and the show begins. Just picture it...

The sun starts to set. Your fans begin to fill the stands as your squad[1] steps on to the track and you finally get to perform the stunts[2] you have practiced all week. You feel a rush of adrenaline as you hear the band start to march on the field proudly playing your fight song. The football team is lined up and ready to break through the banner on center field. And after the playing of the National Anthem, it's kickoff time!

BAND PLAYER

I play bass drums for the marching band, and I love it! Preparing for the next football game is exciting and challenging because you need to learn the different marching commands for the half-time shows: come to attention, march in step – left, right, left, right; execute pivots. It's quite hard to remember as you're playing your instrument, but the crowd's cheers are the best motivation.

1. the squad = the team of cheerleaders
2. a stunt = *une acrobatie*

1 **Take a look at this yearbook* page.**

FRIDAY NIGHT *lights*

a. Guess: what happens on Friday night | what these lights are

b. Look at the pictures of the people involved. Which role do you want to discover?

FOOTBALL PLAYER

We start preparing for the Friday night game on Monday. We train every day, before and after school, to be ready. It's quite hard. But when the Friday night lights illuminate the field and everyone gets together, you understand why you make these sacrifices.

The cheerleaders, the marching band and our coaches all get together on the field to help us deliver our best performances. Fans fill the stands to support and cheer for us. It's the most sensational feeling of community and excitement!

SCHOOL PHOTOGRAPHER

I'm the school photographer at my school and I'm in charge of taking pictures of the Friday night game. It's really challenging because you want to make sure you have beautiful shots of the players' best performances. It's a lot of responsibility and hard work – you need to get there early and be there every Friday. It sometimes rains or snows. But when you see people's joy in reliving the match through your pictures, you realize it's totally worth it.

Extract from a school yearbook

* **A yearbook** is a book that is published by a school each year. It shows the activities at the school during that year.

Work on ONE of these texts

2 IN PAIRS Complete the activities to understand the tradition of Friday night games. WB p. 15-17

3 **What about the spectators?** Sarah, an exchange student, shares her impressions.

a. **Watch Sarah's vlog.**

Video 22nefe5201

What do you think of the atmosphere in her school? Start a wordcloud about it.

exciting sensational ...

b. IN GROUPS **Focus on what Sarah says about:**

the fans and their roles *(group A)*

what happens before and during the game *(group B)*

MINI TASK !

Contribute to a yearbook!

Complete a yearbook page about the Friday night game. WB p. 18

Dans cette leçon, tu as appris :

Vocabulaire » p. 36
- Le sport à l'école

Grammaire » p. 38
- Les déterminants *a(n)/the*
- L'expression de la fréquence

LESSON 2

Off to the Thanksgiving games!

1 Happy Thanksgiving!

Video 22nefe5202

1 **Look at the people. Guess:**

where they are | what they are doing | why they are dressed this way

2 **Watch the first 30 seconds of the video with the sound off.**

a. Were you right?

b. Share what you remember seeing.

3 IN TEAMS **Watch the video with the sound and subtitles on to understand more.** WB p. 19

Thanksgiving

It is a major American holiday celebrated on the 4th Thursday of November. People usually spend it with their family, eat a good meal (roast turkey is a favorite dish!) and watch football games.

History of Thanksgiving

Thanksgiving was originally a holiday to thank God for the harvest*.
The tradition started with the first English people who settled in America in 1620. They organized the first Thanksgiving celebration in 1621. It lasted three days!

* *la récolte*

2 The traditions of the Thanksgiving games

1 **Look at the pictures on p. 33.**
Can you identify what they show?

2 **Camry, an American student, explains the Thanksgiving games.**

a. Read her comments on p. 33.

b. Match them with the correct pictures.

c. Can you explain what the Thanksgiving games are?

a Large family gatherings happen on Thanksgiving. Turkey is the main meat that is served and often a symbol of that particular day.

b Mariah Carey is wearing the home team's colours and is singing the US national anthem. The national anthem plays over the speakers before each game.

c It's a picture of people at tailgate. They are eating and drinking in a parking lot outside of a stadium. They're wearing turkey hats to celebrate Thanksgiving, and wearing their favourite team's colors. Tailgate usually starts 3 to 5 hours before the football game begins. It is a time for socializing with friends and other fans.

d Professional football teams always have a big game on Thanksgiving.

e The cheerleaders are performing for the audience in a stadium.

MINI TASK!

Mime time!

1. **Pick:**
   - a role: cheerleader | athlete | fan | spectator | ...
   - a place: at home | in front of the TV | at the dinner table | at the stadium | ...
   - an action related to a game or family reunion.
2. **Mime it!** Your classmates will have to guess what you are doing.

> You're an athlete!
> You're playing football at the stadium!

Dans cette leçon, tu as appris :

Vocabulaire p. 36
- Les événements sportifs
- La fête de Thanksgiving

Grammaire p. 38
- Le Présent *BE* + V-*ing*

FINAL TASK!

You are spending a month in an American school, just in time for Thanksgiving! Contribute to the school yearbook.

Pense à utiliser le lexique p. 36.

1 Choose the event you want to write about:

- the Thanksgiving game at the city stadium
- the Thanksgiving game at school

2 Select the pictures you want to use.

- You can:
  - cut out the pictures in your WB p. 123
  - draw your own pictures
  - print pictures from the Internet

3 Write a comment for each picture.

Explain what is happening or which tradition the picture illustrates.

4 Organize your pictures and comments.

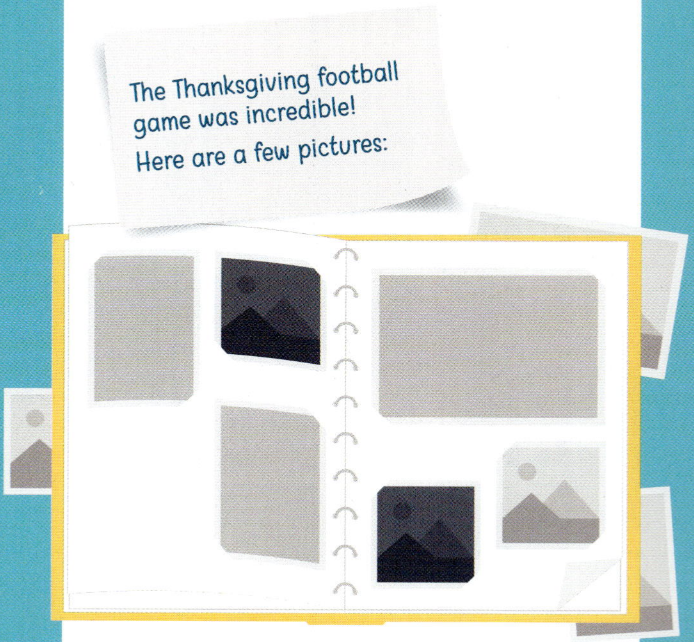

NEED HELP?
Follow the guide!

NEED HELP?

Entraîne-toi à commenter des images.

1 Tu es sur les gradins ! Imagine ce que tu ressens.

Thanksgiving game

+	–
– exciting	– cold (November!)
– ...	– ...

Écris tes idées dans le désordre. S'il te manque du lexique, cherche-le.
→ Words p. 36

2 Choisis tes photos.

Picture 1

– People: ...
– Action: ...
– Your feelings: ...

Prends des notes pour chaque photo.

Si tu es à court d'idées, regarde à nouveau les deux vidéos du chapitre.
Video 22nefe5201
Video 22nefe5202

Picture 2

– ...
– ...
– ...

3 Rédige un court commentaire pour chaque photo.

The band starts to march on the field.

Pour simplement décrire ce qui se passe → Présent simple (p. 25)

These fans are clearly enjoying the game!

Pour commenter / expliquer ce qui se passe → Présent *BE* + V-*ing* (p. 39)

It's cold, **but** we're all having so much fun!

Pour relier deux phrases simples → *but, and, so...*

4 Relis et corrige ton brouillon avant de le recopier.

Vérifie l'orthographe des mots à l'aide du lexique p. 36.
N'oublie pas la ponctuation !

Te voilà fin prêt(e) pour la FINAL TASK!

WORDS

Apprends ces mots avec leur prononciation !

The game

Audio 22nefe5203

play a game
the stands
a field = a pitch
a **mas**cot

a **sta**dium
/'steɪdɪəm/

a fan,
the crowd = *la foule*
cheer, sup**port**
/tʃɪər /
yell = shout
/aʊ/

train, **prac**tise

win ≠ lose

a **cheer**leader

a pho**to**grapher
take / shoot a **pic**ture

Feelings and opinions

- ex**ci**ting = fun
  /ɪk'saɪtɪŋ/
- **chal**lenging = hard, **dif**ficult
- It is worth it!
- There is **no**thing like this!

a band
play an **in**strument,
play the drums
sing the **na**tional **an**them
/'næʃənəl/ /θ/

Team sports

Audio 22nefe5204

(American) **foot**ball

basketball

baseball

hockey

a **pla**yer

a coach

a team
a **team**mate

Thanksgiving traditions

Audio 22nefe5205

celebrate
/selɪbreɪt/

spend time with your **fa**mily
a **fa**mily **ga**thering / get to**ge**ther
be **gra**teful for
a **ho**liday = *un jour férié*

eat **tur**key

a **tur**key

Les événements sportifs

1 ✱ **Guessing game!** **Sauras-tu retrouver qui se cache derrière chacun des rôles décrits ?**

She takes pictures. You'll see them in the yearbook!

He is in charge of instructing the players.

They yell and clap their hands.

They are crowd leaders and athletes.

2 Listen up! Audio 22nefe5206

✱✱ **Tu vas entendre 4 phrases incomplètes. Écoute bien et termine chacune d'entre elles en choisissant le mot ou l'expression qui convient.**

The fans sit in the ...

stands!

3 ✱✱ **Observe bien les silhouettes de joueurs et les logos de ces fédérations de sports très populaires aux États-Unis. Essaie de deviner les noms de ces fédérations !**

Exemple : *MLB* → *Major League Baseball.*

4 ✱✱✱ **Quels noms correspondent aux définitions suivantes ?**

1. a person or a group of young people who shouts out special songs or chants to encourage the team during a game in sports.
2. a person who trains players and makes decisions during games.
3. a large open area with many stands that is used for sports events, concerts, etc.
4. a person, animal, or object used as a symbol to represent a group and bring good luck.

Les fêtes

5 ✱✱ **a. Peux-tu retrouver le nom des éléments suivants ?**

b. Associe chaque élément à une ou plusieurs de ces fêtes :

Halloween | Thanksgiving | Christmas

Sentiments et opinions

6 ✱✱ **On te propose les activités suivantes. Pour chacune, dis ce que tu en penses puis choisis celle que tu préfères.**

1. Let's dance like the cheerleaders!
2. Let's organize a treasure hunt in the stadium!
3. Come and do push-ups with us!
4. Let's run around the track for 20 minutes!

Yes, It's fun!

7 Prononciation Audio 22nefe5207

a. Écoute bien ces mots en faisant attention à l'accentuation. Que remarques-tu ?

cheerleader – **year**book

b. Écoute à présent d'autres noms composés et répète-les.

Thanksgiving – **school** spirit
teammate – **band** player
baseball – **bas**ketball – **foot**ball

Ces noms sont constitués de deux mots, on les appelle des noms composés : ***team**mate*
→ *Grammar* p. 54

Accentuation des noms composés

En anglais, les noms composés sont le plus souvent accentués sur le premier élément : **cheer**leader - **year**book

Poursuis l'entraînement
WB p. 20

Les déterminants : *the / a(n)*

Pour parler d'éléments définis ou non définis, on emploie différents déterminants :

article indéfini *a(n)* : pour présenter un élément nouveau ou non défini. Ici, il s'agit de n'importe quelle cheerleader.

The main role of a cheerleader is to get the whole school excited about the game [...].

article défini *the* : présente un élément précis, déterminé. Ici, il s'agit de l'école de la cheerleader évoquée juste avant, et du match prévu.

- *the* s'emploie au singulier et au pluriel. Il n'a pas de genre (masculin/féminin).
- *a(n)* s'emploie devant un nom dénombrable singulier. Il n'a pas de genre non plus.
- On emploie *a* devant un son consonne et *an* devant un son voyelle : *an athlete*

1 ★ C'est la rentrée ! **Complète la liste de courses de cette cheerleader à l'aide du déterminant *a* ou *an*.**

For my equipment:

.... green skirt
.... orange and white top
.... hair bow
.... yellow cheer bag
.... large megaphone
.... pair of white socks
.... American flag

2 ★★ **Tu as envie de découvrir la série *Friday Night Lights* ? Complète ce petit résumé à l'aide de *a* ou *the*.**

1. ... series follows ... high school football team in ... fictional town of Texas.
2. Eric Taylor is ... new football coach for ... "Dillon Panthers".
3. It is based on ... book "*Friday Night Lights: A Town, ... Team and ... Dream*".

L'expression de la fréquence

Pour préciser que l'on fait quelque chose parfois, souvent, toujours, etc., on utilise des adverbes de fréquence.

It sometimes rains or snows.

We always wear a spirit shirt.

Ils se placent généralement devant le verbe, sauf avec *BE* : → *I'm often on time.*

never – sometimes – often – usually – always

3 ★★ **Devine ce que fait cette cheerleader pour rester en forme ? Complète ses phrases à l'aide de :**
always – sometimes – often

I have a healthy breakfast.

In my free time, I go swimming.

I train after school.

4 ★★★ **C'est le début de l'année ! Complète le discours de la coach à ses joueurs à l'aide d'adverbes de fréquence.**

Ok, so this year is crucial: we *must* win the championship! So, here is some advice: ... arrive on time for practice! ... forget to do your exercises! You can ... eat pizza but ... before a game! ... remember to eat a good healthy meal the day before.

LESSON 2

Le Présent *BE* + V-*ing*

Tu as vu que le Présent simple permet de donner une information (→ p. 23). Lorsque l'on veut faire « plus » que cela (par exemple expliquer, commenter...), on utilise le présent *BE* + *V-ing*.

What are they doing?

The cheerleaders are performing in a stadium.

Luckily, it is not raining.

↑ *BE* au Présent — base verbale + -*ing*

I'm singing	We're singing
You're singing	You're singing
He/She/It's singing	They're singing

- *BE* passe devant **le sujet** dans les questions :
  → *Is* ***the crowd*** *cheering?*
- Il est suivi de la marque de la **négation** :
  → *I'm* ***not*** *listening.*
- Il est repris dans les réponses brèves :
  → *Are you listening? No, I'm not.*

Attention à l'orthographe !
dance → dancing
run → running
(verbe d'une syllabe terminé par consonne-voyelle-consonne → on double la consonne finale)

1 ✱ Le match de basketball est retransmis à la radio, mais le micro grésille ! Complète ces commentaires en mettant les verbes au Présent *BE* + V-*ing*.

"And the fans are ready to watch the game! Some ___ (*stand*), others ___ (*dance*). Oh and now the cheerleaders ___ (*enter*) the stadium! Get ready for some acrobatics! There it is: the girls ___ (*make*) the most amazing pyramid, you should see that! And now our beloved Ms Pennick … (*sing*) the national anthem. It's wonderful, no wonder the public ___ (*clap*). Ah, the players and the referee ___ (*get*) ready. Let the game begin!"

2 ✱ Que font ces personnages ? Prépare des questions pour voir si tes camarades pensent comme toi.

Is she...or ... ?

Are they ... ?

Is he... ?

1 2 3 4

3 ✱✱ Ambiance de folie pour le match des *Los Angeles Lakers* contre les *Trail Blazers* de Portland, et c'est toi le commentateur radio ! Imagine ce qui se passe.

The fans are ...

4 Prononciation

Audio 22nefe5208

a. Écoute bien ces phrases en faisant attention à la prononciation des verbes. Que remarques-tu ?

1. The chearleaders are per**for**ming.
2. The players are **run**ning around the stadium.

b. Entraîne-toi à prononcer ces phrases.

Prononciation des verbes en -*ing*.
Le "g" à la fin de la terminaison -*ing* est presque muet car c'est la base verbale qui est accentuée :
playing – cheering

Poursuis l'entraînement
WB p. 22-23

Choose your activities!

Early finishers

Sports riddle!

Why did the Pharaoh like cheerleaders?

Because they made a pyramid.

Ron's coach has five players: four are named Jojo, Koko, Lolo and Momo. What is the fifth player's name?

Ron, of course!

Quiz Cheerleading

front craddle

1 **What is considered the cheer capital of the United States?**

a. Texas
b. Minnesota
c. Nevada

Did you know about... National Football League mascots?

Minnesota Vikings

Chicago Bears

San Francisco 49ers

Denver Broncos

Almost every NFL team has a designated mascot. Mascots get people pumped up at sporting events. They choreograph dance routines*, perform, and sometimes they participate with cheerleaders. They also get the crowd excited before and after games by posing for pictures, signing autographs, etc.

* routine = *chorégraphie*

Miles

Viktor

→ **Can you match each of these NFL teams with its mascot?**

→ **Think of a mascot for your school team :-)**

2 **Which US president was a cheerleader?**
a. Barack Obama
b. Abe Lincoln
c. George W. Bush

3 **Which of the following is a normal length for a cheer routine?**
a. Around 3 minutes
b. Around 10 minutes
c. Around 25 seconds

4 **What sport is the number one cause of catastrophic injuries in female athletes?**
a. Gymnastics
b. Cheerleading
c. Soccer

basket tosses

5 **In high school cheerleading (as opposed to competitive cheerleading) you cannot:**
a. do tumbling
b. perform front cradle
c. do basket tosses

tumbling

Answers: 1. a - 2. c - 3. a - 4. b - 5. c

Sourdough Sam

Staley Da Bear

Thanksgiving scavenger hunt

→ **Find as many items related to Thanksgiving as possible. Show them to your teacher and earn Thanksgiving points!**

- something you are thankful for
- something the color of cranberries
- a yellow or orange leaf
- an object that rhymes with the word "turkey"
- something that smells good
- the score of the Thanskgiving game between the Lions and the Bears in Detroit this year
- a nice picture of a Thanksgiving dinner

READING CORNER

Première lecture autonome en anglais ? Pas de panique !

Accepte de ne pas tout comprendre. Pense à t'appuyer sur les images, notamment l'expression des visages, et sur les mots que tu connais.

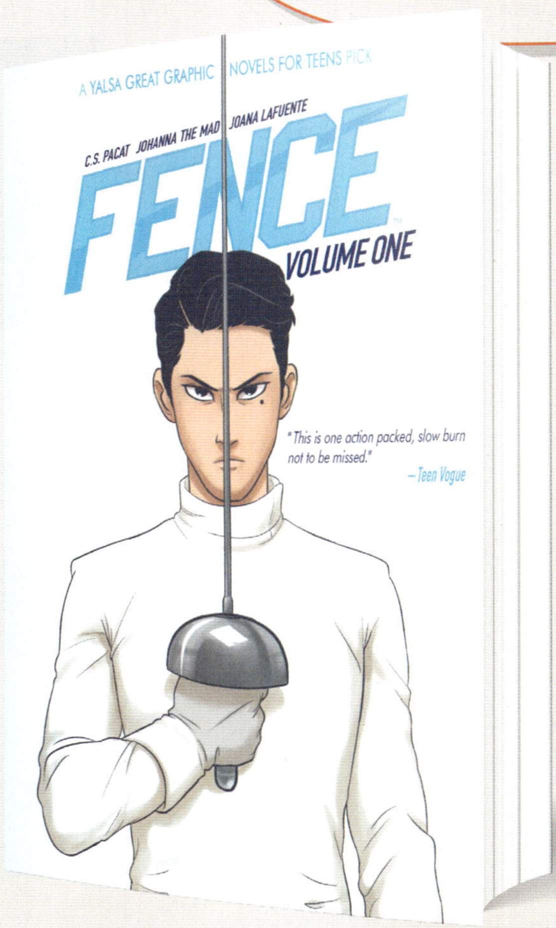

Fence, Boom!Box, 2020

circuit = *tournoi*

HELP

Observe la dernière vignette et rassemble les indices pour comprendre le sentiment de la femme : l'expression de son visage, les mots en gras dans son discours et la ponctuation. Qu'en penses-tu ?

PICK AN ACTIVITY

- **Imagine** who Seiji Katayama is.
- **Draw** the next frame!
- **Act out** the dialogue between Nicholas and the woman.

HELP

Écoute certains mots de la page et entraîne-toi à les prononcer avant de jouer !

Audio 22nefe5209

To be continued on p. 58

PROJECT

3

Your house at school

Dans ce chapitre, tu vas :

- Découvrir les « maisons » d'un collège londonien et les personnalités dont elles portent le nom
- Imaginer à ton tour une « maison » et des compétitions inter-maisons

Vocabulaire

- L'école
- Les éléments d'une biographie

Grammaire

- Les noms composés
- *There is / There are*
- Le Prétérit simple, forme affirmative

JEU NUMÉRIQUE
Snakes & ladders

Hogwarts* isn't the only school with houses. Other British schools have them too!

* *In French:* Poudlard

LESSON 1

School houses

1 Your own house... at school!

A girls' school in West London

1. **The girls on p. 44-45 study at NHEHS** *(see picture of this school above)*. **Can you imagine why they're wearing different colours?**

2. **Watch a video about this school.** Video 22nefe5301
   a. Check if you were right.
   b. IN GROUPS What do you learn about the house system?
   In teams, focus on the following:

The house system
- What it is
- What the objective is
- How the pupils are sorted into the houses

Time to write

Imagine you're a student at NHEHS. Write a short paragraph for the school website to present the house system.

i

The origin of school houses

- This very English tradition started in boarding schools* where pupils spent the school year away from their parents.
- They were put into groups called "houses" to help them feel more at home and to give them a sense of belonging.

* *pensionnats*

2 Discover house competitions!

♥ 51 Likes

nhehs.houses 💚❤️ HOUSE CAPTAINS 2021-22!! 💛💙

Hi everyone!

We are SO excited to be your house captains this year! We hope you enjoyed our first whole school house assembly. REMEMBER KEEP EARNING THOSE HOUSE POINTS and stay tuned for some upcoming events/competitions…

1 Look at this Instagram post. Find out:

who the girls are | what news they want to share

2 IN GROUPS **Work on one of these videos and discover the captains of a house.** Videos 22nefe5302

Use what you have learned to complete your spidergram (p. 46).

The house system

- The houses at NHEHS
  - house colours
  - house captains (names, qualities)

3 Watch the video again.

Focus on the house competitions that are mentioned.

a. Try to list them.

b. Use the name of each competition to guess what it is about.

c. Share with the class.

4 Discover more about house competitions.

Complete the activities in your workbook. WB p. 25-26

5 What do you think of the house system? Discuss!

MINI TASK!

House captain elections IN PAIRS

Run for election as the new captains of one of the NHEHS houses.

1. Introduce yourselves (name, age, role).
2. Present new exciting competitions! They can be fun, ambitious or completely eccentric. *Need help?* WB p. 26
3. Class: vote for your new house captains!

Dans cette leçon, tu as appris :

Vocabulaire ≫ p. 52
- L'école

Grammaire ≫ p. 54
- *There is / There are*
- Les noms composés

LESSON 2

Remarkable women

1 Naming the houses

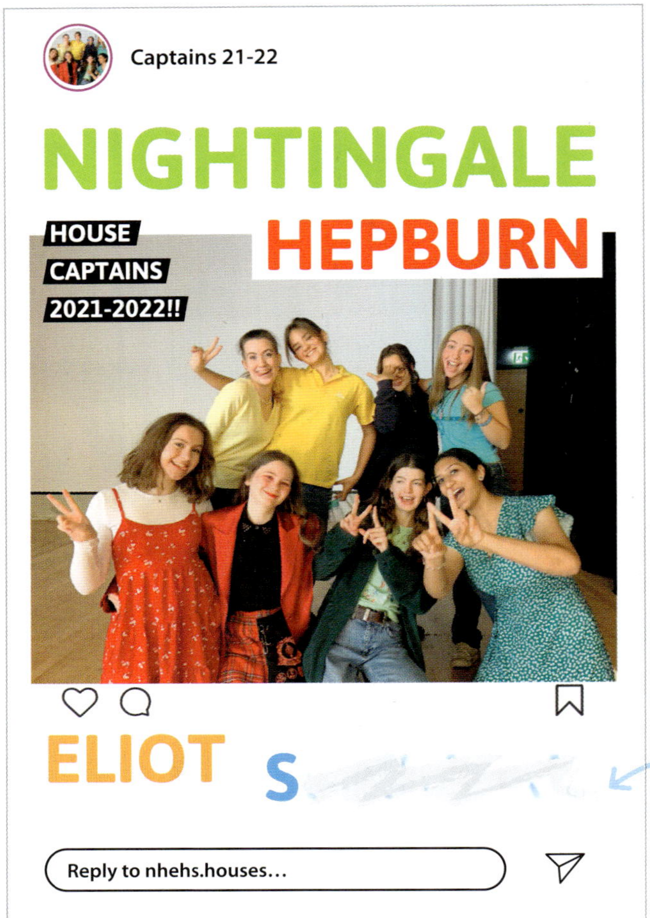

Discover this mysterious name later.

1. **Look at this Instagram post.** Focus on the four coloured words. How can you link them to:
   - the houses at NHEHS
   - the school's name, NHEHS ?
2. Can you guess how the houses' names were chosen?

No luck with our guessing game? Use a joker: ask your teacher for a clue 😊

2 The ladies behind the names

1. **Look at the pictures on p. 49.** Can you guess these women's jobs?
2. **Read the biographies on p. 49.** Try to match each of them with the right picture. Were you right about their jobs?
3. IN GROUPS **Choose one biography.**
   a. Read it again and complete the activities in your workbook. WB p. 27-28
   b. In your opinion, why is this woman remarkable?

Time to write You are one of the house captains at NHEHS. Write a tweet to explain the name of your house and why it is a good choice. *Need help?* WB p. 28

1

2

3

A

George **ELIOT**

Mary Ann (Marian) EVANS
(22 November 1819 – 22 December 1880)

Better known by her pen name, George Eliot was an English novelist, poet, journalist and translator. She was one of the leading writers of the Victorian era*.
Middlemarch is perhaps her most famous book and is often considered among the greatest novels in the English language.

* *the time when Queen Victoria reigned (1837-1901).*

B

Florence **NIGHTINGALE**

(12 May 1820 – 13 August 1910)

An English nurse. She helped create the modern techniques of nursing. She became a leader of the team of nurses who helped wounded soldiers during the Crimean War (1853-56)*.
As a nurse, she was given the name 'The Lady with the Lamp' because at night, she checked on the wounded soldiers and always carried 'The Lamp' with her.

* *a war between Russia on one side, and Britain, France and Turkey on the other side.*

C

Audrey **HEPBURN**

(4 May 1929 – 20 January 1993)

A British actress, fashion icon, and humanitarian admired for her charm and elegance. She starred in classic films such as *Roman Holiday* (1956) and *Breakfast at Tiffany's* (1961). Hepburn is one of the few actresses who won an Emmy, Tony, Grammy and Academy Award. She became an ambassador for UNICEF in the late 1980s. Her work to help children around the world continues today.

Adapted from kiddle.co

MINI TASK!

Choose a name for the fourth house IN PAIRS

1. It is time to find the name of the house that starts with an S. Who do you want to choose? Spencer, Shelley or Sharman?
2. Read these women's biographies in your workbook and complete the activities. WB p. 29-30
3. Vote: which woman does your class prefer?

Check with your teacher: did NHEHS make the same choice as you?

Dans cette leçon, tu as appris :

Vocabulaire p. 52
- Les éléments d'une biographie

Grammaire p. 55
- Le Prétérit simple, forme affirmative

FINAL TASK!

IN GROUPS

Create your own houses at school!

Pense à utiliser le lexique p. 52.

1 Choose a name for your house.

- Think about a remarkable person from an English-speaking country.
  This person can be: an artist | a leader | an athlete | a famous chef | ...
- Read about his or her life and select what you want to tell the class.

You can use kids.kiddle.co

2 Choose your house colour and emblem.

- Choose a colour 
- Design an emblem... free your creativity!

3 Present your house.

- Choose two captains for the house.
- House captains: introduce yourselves and present your house to the class: name, biography of the remarkable person, colour, emblem....

- Captains: don't forget to wear your house captain badge!
- Team: don't forget to wear your house colour(s)!

4 Present your house competitions.

- Team: suggest fun competitions and events!
- Class: vote for your favourite events!

Why not carry your school house project for the whole year?

NEED HELP? Follow the guide!

NEED HELP?

Apprends à te documenter en vue d'une présentation

1 Recherche les informations utiles.

a. Recherche une biographie de la personne que tu as choisie. Tu peux utiliser le site kids.kiddle.co.

b. Repère les informations principales.

Valerie Jane
MORRIS-GOODALL (1934-)

A British primatologist* and anthropologist* best known as the leading expert on chimpanzees. Goodall made important discoveries about chimpanzee social and family life, notably that chimps eat meat, use tools and have different personalities. She is a leader in the protection of chimpanzees and their habitats.
Time magazine named Goodall as one of the 100 most influential people in the world in 2019.

Adapted from kids.kiddle.co

Trouve une image qui illustre bien la vie de la personnalité que tu as choisie.

* Si tu ne connais pas un mot, tu peux :
– cliquer dessus s'il est en **couleur**,
– utiliser un dictionnaire en ligne (learnersdictionary.com, wordreference.com – tu pourras ainsi l'entendre prononcé !).

2 Prépare tes notes.

a. Sélectionne les informations importantes.

→ British anthropologist / expert on chimpanzees, ...

b. Prépare tes notes.

Écris les dates en toutes lettres si cela peut t'aider à les prononcer.

Procède sous forme de liste et ne rédige pas tout !

- Jane Goodall (1934 / nineteen thirty-four)
- Primatologist / anthropologist
- Best known for: being an expert on chimpanzees

3 Entraîne-toi à parler à partir de tes notes. Audio 22nefe5303

Vérifie la prononciation et l'accentuation.

Our house is named after Jane Goodall.
/eɪ/ /eɪ/ /ɔ:/

She was born in **nine**teen thirty-four and
/aɪ/ /ɜ:/ /ɔ:/

she is a **Bri**tish prima**to**logist and anthro**po**logist.
/ɪ/ /aɪ/ /dʒ/ /ɵ/

She is a great **ex**pert on chimpan**zees**.
/eɪ/ /ɜ:/ /tʃ/ /i:z/

Enregistre-toi et écoute-toi pour pouvoir t'améliorer.

Fais des phrases courtes : Sujet – Verbe – Complément

Te voilà fin prêt(e) pour la FINAL TASK !

WORDS

Apprends ces mots avec leur prononciation !

At school

Audio 22nefe5304

pupil (UK)
student (US)

school house
house captain
/ɪn/
house com**pe**titions

School clubs

chess club
/tʃ/

sports club
Spanish club
French club
video **games** club
film club

knitting club
/nɪ/

drama club

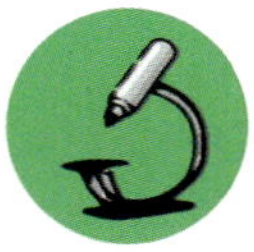

science club
/aɪ/

Professions

Audio 22nefe5305

an **ac**tor / an **ac**tress
a **wri**ter, a **po**et
/aɪ/ /pəʊɪt/
a **jour**nalist
a his**to**rian
an ex**plo**rer
an **as**tronaut
a poli**ti**cian
a **pi**lot
/aɪ/

a **sci**entist
/aɪ/

an **ath**lete

a mu**si**cian

a **pain**ter

a **tea**cher

a **nurse**
/ɜː/
a **doc**tor
/ə/

En anglais, on emploie un article indéfini quand on évoque le métier de quelqu'un :
→ *She is* *__an__* ***extraor****dinary* ***sports****woman.*
He was *__a__* ***fa****mous* ***po****et.*

Remarkable people

Audio 22nefe5306

ex**traor**dinary **ad**mirable re**mar**kable **me**morable **fa**mous
/ɪ/

 be born –  be**come** –  die

She was born __in__ 1889 __on__ the 5th of **Au**gust.

cre**ate** / in**vent** – change the world – make a **ground**breaking dis**co**very – be a pio**neer** in…
/aʊ/ /eɪ/ /paɪə'nɪə/

Dates

Audio 22nefe5307

in the Vic**to**rian **e**ra
during the war

on the 12th of May 1820
(eigh**teen twen**ty)

1800 → 1899

in the **ear**ly 19th **cen**tury ≠ in the late 19th **cen**tury

2022

On lit d'abord les deux premiers chiffres : **twen**ty
puis les deux derniers : **twen**ty-two

À l'école

1 ✱✱ **Quelle chance, tu passes un an à NHEHS ! Dis ce que tu aimerais y faire :**

I'd like to be…

I'd like to join…

Responsibilities	Clubs
…	…

2 Prononciation Audio 22nefe5308

a. **Écoute ces noms composés en faisant attention à l'accentuation. Que remarques-tu ?**

house points **school** house

b. **Écoute d'autres noms composés et répète-les.**

head boy **house** captain **chess** club

c. **Écoute-les employés dans des phrases et répète ces phrases.**

L'accentuation des noms composés

En anglais, les noms composés sont le plus souvent accentués sur le premier élément du mot : ***house*** *points*.

Les métiers

3 Dictation time! Audio 22nefe5309

✱ **Écoute six noms de métiers. Écris-les dans ton cahier en faisant attention à l'orthographe. Puis entoure celui qui te plairait le plus.**

4 ✱✱ **Joue au scrabble avec un(e) camarade en utilisant les mots du chapitre. Combien de mots parviendrez-vous à placer ?**

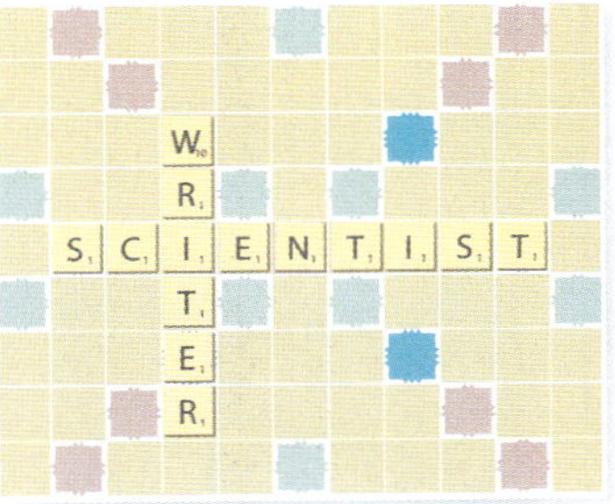

5 ✱✱✱ **Trouve les métiers définis ci-dessous :**

1. a person who takes care of injured people. → a …
2. a person who studies science. → …
3. a person who writes books. → …
4. a person who travels in a spacecraft. → …

Les grands personnages

6 ✱ **Raconte la vie de Graham Bell, l'inventeur du téléphone. Complète les phrases avec les verbes suivants :**

became

invented

was born

died

Graham Bell in 1892

1. Alexander Graham Bell … in 1847 in Scotland.
2. At the age of sixteen, he … a teacher of elocution and music.
3. In 1876, Bell … the telephone.
4. He … in 1922.

Les dates

7 ✱✱ **Voici les dates de naissance de personnes célèbres, telles qu'on les dirait à l'oral.**

1. July twenty-third nineteen eighty-nine
2. April twenty-sixth fifteen sixty-four
3. the twenty-first of April nineteen twenty-six
4. the eighteenth of June nineteen forty-two

a. **Associe chacune à une date en chiffres :**

a 

b 

c 

d 

b. **Qui se cache derrière chaque date ?**

Queen Elizabeth II — Daniel Radcliffe — Paul McCartney — William Shakespeare

8 Dictation time! Audio 22nefe5310

a. ✱✱ **Tu vas entendre citer cinq périodes de l'histoire. Écris-les dans ton cahier.**

b. **Peux-tu les classer dans l'ordre chronologique ?**

Poursuis l'entraînement WB p. 31

There is… / There are…

Pour indiquer ce qu'il y a quelque part, on peut utiliser *there is* ou *there are*.

There are four houses at NHEHS.

There is a new student in our house.

Le verbe ***BE*** s'accorde avec le premier nom (ou nom composé) qui le suit.

There → **is** + (premier nom **singulier**)
There → **are** + (premier nom **pluriel**)

1 ★ **Le début de ces phrases a disparu ! Complète-les avec *there is* ou *there are*.**

1. … many house competitions at NHEHS.
2. For example, … a singing competition every term and a sports day once a year.
3. And I love NHEHS because … very nice girls there.

2 ★★ **Quels clubs y a-t-il dans cette école ? Écoute et identifie l'affiche qui les illustre.**

Audio 22nefe5311

① ② ③

3 ★★ IN PAIRS **Find the odd one out!**

a. **Nomme les clubs qu'il y a dans l'école de tes rêves.**

b. **Ajoute un intrus. Ton ou ta camarade saura-t-il / elle le trouver ?**

In my dream school, there…

Les noms composés

Certains noms sont composés de deux noms, le premier précisant le sens du second.

There are two house captains.

- house : **Nom qui apporte une précision** — Il ne s'accorde pas.
- captains : **Nom principal** — Il prend la marque du pluriel.

4 ★ **Complète les phrases en plaçant les noms dans le bon ordre :**

specialist - chimpanzee	1. Jane Goodall is a … .
space - mission	2. Helen Sharman had her first … on May 18, 1991.
club - science chess - club	3. In our school, there is a … and a … .

5 ★★ **Propose des activités pour une journée de compétitions dans ton école ! Forme le maximum de noms composés à partir des mots suivants et illustre-les :**

scrabble — art — jungle — gardening — costume — swamp football — ugly Christmas sweater

show — match — contest — race — competition — marathon

Exemple :

jungle marathon

swamp football …

a. **Combien de compétitions as-tu inventées ?**

b. **Lesquelles te semblent les plus enthousiasmantes ? Les plus excentriques ?**

LESSON 2

Le Prétérit simple (forme affirmative)

Le Prétérit simple permet de parler d'événements passés et révolus.

Audrey Hepburn starr**ed** in classic films.

Pour un verbe **régulier**, on ajoute la terminaison *-ed* à la base verbale, à toutes les personnes.

She **became** an ambassador for UNICEF.

Le Prétérit des verbes **irréguliers** est différent : il faut l'apprendre par cœur ! → Liste p. 158
La forme reste la même à toutes les personnes.

⚠ carry + *-ed* → carried
create + *-ed* → created

Comment utiliser *BE* au Prétérit ?
***BE* est le seul verbe irrégulier à avoir deux formes au Prétérit :**

Audrey Hepburn **was** a British actress.

These three women **were** remarkable.

I was
You were
He, she, it was
We were
You were
They were

1 ★ Ton professeur t'a demandé de raconter la vie d'Anna Pavlova.

N'oublie pas de mettre les verbes au Prétérit !

1. Anna Pavlova ... a British ballerina of the early 20th century. *(be)*
2. She ... born in Russia in 1881. *(be)*
3. Pavlova ... one of the finest classical ballet dancers. *(become)*
4. She ... *The Dying Swan*, a short ballet, about 4,000 times. *(dance)*
5. Pavlova ... in London from 1912 until her death in 1931. *(live)*

Anna Pavlova, 1912

2 Dictation time! Audio 22nefe5312

★★ **Écoute ces phrases puis complète-les.**

1. Stephen Hawking ... on 8th January 1942.
2. He ... not a very good pupil at first.
3. With time, he ... very good at science and later, he ... physics.
4. He ... a great cosmologist and ... the universe.
5. He ... a lot of scientific prizes and ... in an episode of *Star Trek* and even in one of *The Simpsons*.
6. He ... on 14th March 2018.

3 ★★★ IN PAIRS Play two truths and a lie!

a. Écris trois phrases à propos de ta vie passée : deux doivent être vraies et la troisième une pure invention. Ton ou ta camarade saura-t-il/elle la trouver ?

b. Et toi, sauras-tu identifier le mensonge inventé par ton ou ta camarade ?

4 Prononciation Audio 22nefe5313

a. Écoute ces verbes conjugués au Prétérit. Entraîne-toi à les prononcer.

helped	starred	created
/t/	/d/	/ɪd/

b. Écoute d'autres verbes et classe-les selon la prononciation de leur terminaison :

checked – edited – died – worked – acted – played – studied – invented – organized – received

/t/	/d/	/ɪd/
...	...	...

La terminaison *-ed* du Prétérit
Elle se prononce de trois façons différentes, selon le son qui la précède.

Poursuis l'entraînement
WB p. 33

Choose your activities!

Early finishers

Quiz

Which Hogwarts house do you belong to?

1. **Pick one word to describe yourself:**
   - a. brave = courageous
   - b. determined
   - c. patient
   - d. clever = intelligent

2. **What's your favourite colour?**
   - a. red
   - b. green
   - c. yellow
   - d. blue

Did you know about... the oldest school in Europe?

The King's school, located in Canterbury, UK, was founded in 597! It is the oldest school in Europe and the second-oldest school in the world. First created as an all-boys school, admission for female students opened in the 1970s.

Guess where the oldest school in the world is:
a. Germany – b. Marocco – c. China

c. The oldest school in the world still in use today was founded between 143-141 BC in Chengdu, China.

School Joke!

→ On the first day of school, the teacher asked a student, "What are your parents' names?" The student replied, "My father's name is Laughing and my mother's name is Smiling." The teacher said, "Are you kidding*?" The student said, "No, Kidding is my brother. I am Joking."

* kid *(v.)* = *plaisanter*

Weird but true

Balliol College and Trinity College are long-time rivals at Oxford University. Every year, to see which of them is the best in England, they organize a very special race*.

* *une course*

Can you guess what sort of race it is?
- a. a tortoise race
- b. a rabbit race
- c. a horse race

b. a tortoise race

Sorting hat!

3 **What's your favourite animal?**
a. lion
b. snake
c. badger*
d. eagle

4 **How do you enjoy spending your free time?**
a. practising sport
b. playing video games
c. spending time with friends
d. reading a book

5 **How do you feel about English?**
a. It's fun.
b. It's very hard.
c. It's easy.
d. I don't like it.

* badger = *blaireau*

6 **What's your favourite class?**
a. Art
b. History
c. PE (Physical Education)
d. Maths

7 **What's your ideal place to be?**
a. woods
b. dungeon
c. kitchen
d. library

8 **Finally, what's your dream job?**
a. athlete
b. politician
c. scientist
d. writer

Find out which Hogwarts House you are in! Audio 22nefe5322

School years around the world

UK	FRANCE	AUSTRALIA
School year:	**School year:**	**School year:**
• 190 days	• 180 days	• 200 days
• From early September to mid or late July	• From early September to early July	• From early February to mid December

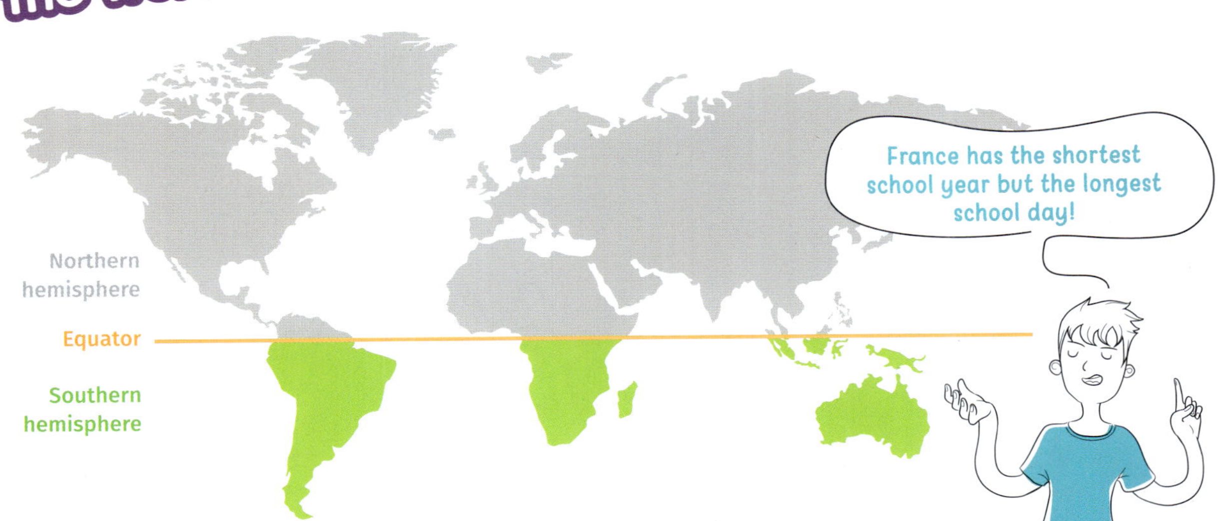

→ **When is the summer vacation in Australia?**
Can you explain why? Can you locate Australia?

READING CORNER

Previously in *FENCE* ...

Nicholas will compete against Seiji. But first, he has to face the other competitors...

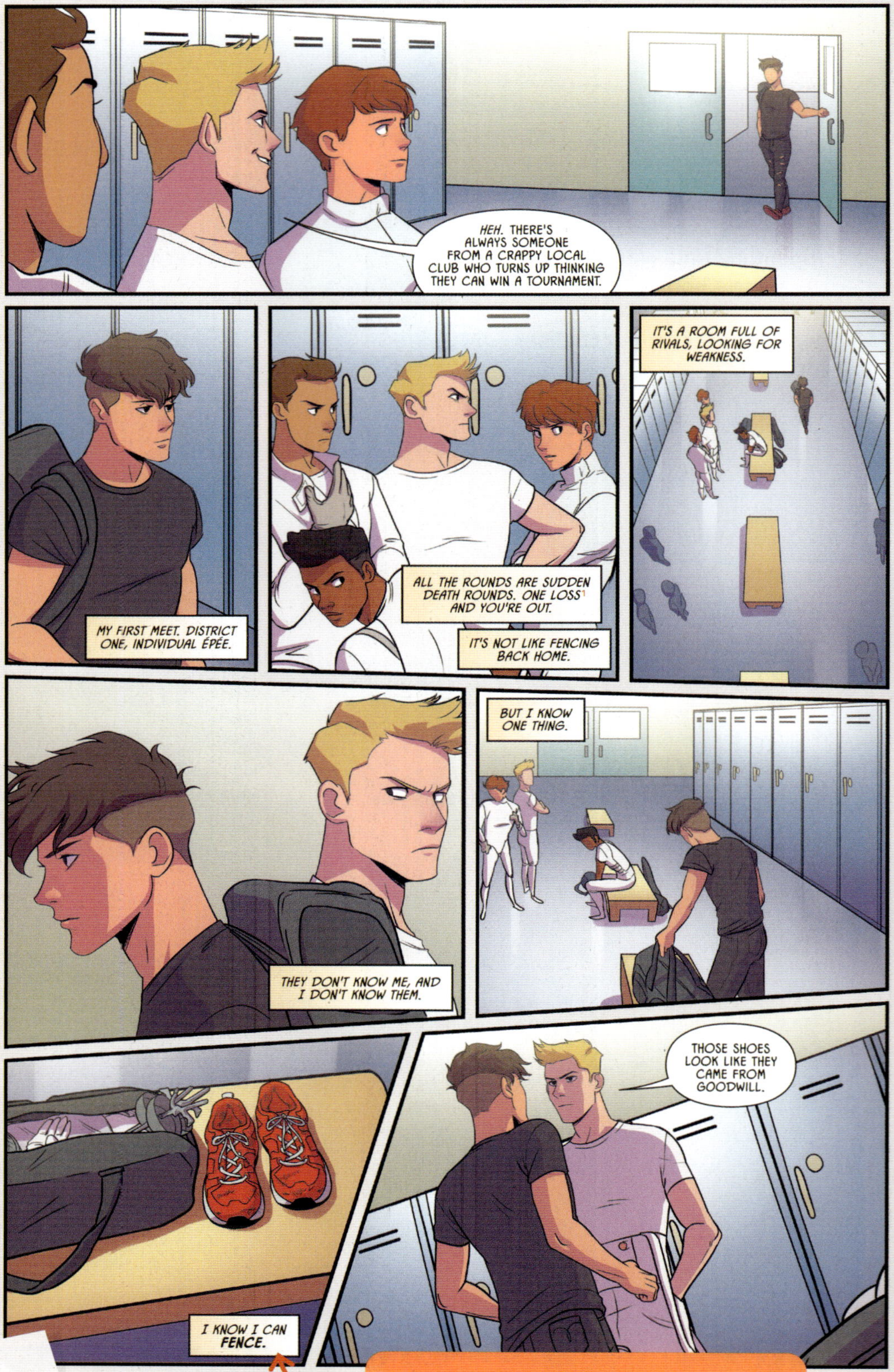

Que révèle cette pensée concernant le caractère de Nicholas ?

1. one loss = *une défaite*
2. leave it = *laisse tomber*

HELP

- Les cadres sur fond jaune pâle reflètent les pensées de Nicholas :

I KNOW I CAN FENCE.

- tandis que les bulles blanches sont les répliques des personnages :

NICE KNOWING YOU.

- Observe bien l'expression des visages des personnages : quels sont leurs sentiments à ton avis ? Que ressentent-ils les uns envers les autres ?

PICK AN ACTIVITY

Imagine an answer to Nicholas's final question.

WHAT'S SO GOOD ABOUT THIS SEIJI GUY, ANYWAY?

Imagine what Seiji looks like and draw the next vignette.

To be continued on p. 74

PROJECT

4

Choose Kindness

Dans ce chapitre, tu vas :

- Découvrir un roman jeunesse sur le thème de la tolérance
- Apprendre à écrire un dialogue pour raconter une histoire

Vocabulaire

- Personnalité et sentiments
- Les relations avec les autres

Grammaire

- Le pronom relatif *who*
- Les pronoms personnels compléments
- Les questions au Prétérit simple

JEU NUMÉRIQUE

The Emotions board game

Discover an American bestseller for teens!

LESSON 1

Meet August

1 An ordinary kid?

1 **Look at the film poster.**
What can you guess about the characters? List your ideas.

2 **Read the text.**
In your opinion, which character from the poster is the narrator?

3 **What do you learn about this character?**
Work on the text in your workbook.
WB p. 36

THE NARRATOR
- Name:
- ...
- ...

4 **Recap.**

I feel ordinary. Inside.

Why "inside"? Explain.

ORDINARY

I know I'm not an ordinary ten-year-old kid. I mean, I'm sure, I do ordinary things. I eat ice cream. I ride my bike. I play ball. I have an XBox. Stuff like that makes me ordinary. I guess. And I feel ordinary. Inside. But I know ordinary kids don't make other ordinary kids run away screaming in playgrounds. I know ordinary kids don't get stared at* wherever they go. [...]

My name is August, by the way. I won't describe what I look like. Whatever you're thinking, it's probably worse.

Wonder, R.J. Palacio, 2012

* stare at (somebody): *dévisager*

2 A special day

1 **Watch the beginning of the *Wonder* trailer with the sound off** (0' - 1'09).

Video 22nefe5401

Say what you understand about the situation:

place | time of year | people

HELP

Appuie-toi sur les mots accentués pour comprendre ce qui est dit :
– *real school*
– *surgeries*
– *totally petrified*
– ...

IN GROUPS

2 **Watch the video with the sound on.**

a. Check and complete your answers to question 1. WB p. 36

b. Share with the other groups.

3 **Choose a character.**

a. Identify their attitude and feelings. Can you imagine why they feel this way? WB p. 37

b. Share with the class.

4 **Now read this extract from a study guide.**

Do the activity in your workbook. WB p. 37

WONDER CHARACTER LIST

This is ISABEL PULLMAN, who is Auggie's mother. She loves Auggie deeply and truly. She wants the best for him but can sometimes be overprotective.

Adapted from: *Wonder Study Guide*, gradesaver.com

Time to write IN PAIRS Complete the study guide for other characters. WB p. 38

MINI TASK!

Contribute to the *Wonder* character list.

Write a short paragraph to introduce August.
Think about:

his relationship with his family | his school life | his personality | his feelings

WB p. 38

Dans cette leçon, tu as appris :

Vocabulaire p. 68
- Les adjectifs de personnalité
- Les sentiments

Grammaire p. 70
- Le pronom relatif *who*
- Les pronoms personnels compléments

LESSON 2

Ups and downs

1 A day in the life of Auggie

"SO, IT WENT OK?"

A new day of school is over. Auggie just said goodbye to his friend Summer. Now, he meets his mother who is picking him up.

"So it went okay?" said Mom. I could tell she had a million questions she wanted to ask me. "Everyone was nice? Did you like your teachers?"

"Yeah."

"How about those kids you met last week? Were they nice?"

"Fine, fine. Jack hung out with me a lot."

"That's so great, sweetie. What about that boy Julian?"

I thought about that Darth Sidious comment[1]. By now it felt like that happened a hundred years ago.

"He was okay," I said.

"And the blond girl, what was her name?"

"Charlotte. Mom, I said everyone was nice already."

"Okay," Mom answered.

I honestly don't know why I was kind of mad at Mom[2], but I was. We crossed Amesfort Avenue, and she didn't say anything else until we turned onto our block.

"So," Mom said. "How did you meet Summer if she wasn't in any of your classes?"

"We sat together at lunch," I said. I had started kicking a rock between my feet like it was a soccer ball, chasing it back and forth across the sidewalk.

"She seems very nice."

"Yeah, she is."

"She's very pretty," Mom said.

"Yeah, I know," I answered. "We're kind of like Beauty and the Beast."

Wonder, R.J. Palacio, 2012

Your mission

Discover a new extract from *Wonder* and perform a few lines with a friend. Get ready... like an actor!

1. Darth Sidious comment: *commentaire dans lequel Julian comparait August à un personnage effrayant du film Star Wars*
2. *"j'étais un peu en colère contre maman"*

1. **Read the introduction. Make sure you understand:**
   where and when the scene takes place | who is present in the scene

2. **Read the first lines. Make sure you know who is speaking.**
   Highlight each character's lines in your workbook. WB p. 39-40

3. **Read the text methodically.** WB p. 39-40
   a. Identify: the subject of the conversation | the characters' emotions
   b. Share with the class. Did you all understand the same things?

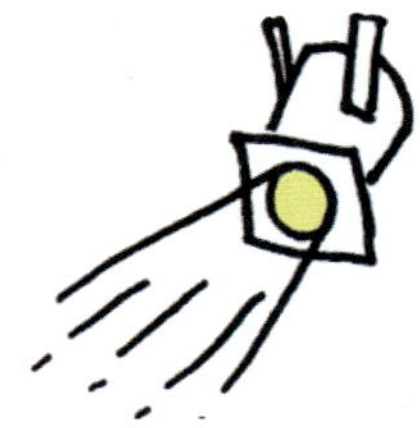

4. IN PAIRS **Act out the scene!**
   a. Decide how much of the scene you are going to play.
   LEVEL 1 line 1 to 5 | LEVEL 2 line 1 to 14 | LEVEL 3 the full text!
   b. Listen to the audio version, rehearse... and perform! Audio 22nefe5402

Time to write Imagine two more questions Auggie's mother could ask him, as well as Auggie's answers. Think about:
his lunch | the classes he had | the people he met | ...

2 Choose kind

1. **Look at the picture. Compare it with the film poster on p. 62.**
   a. What is different?
   b. Choose one adjective to describe the atmosphere in this class.

Auggie's class picture

2. **Watch the end of the trailer.** Video 22nefe5401
   a. Concentrate on:
   the music | the characters' attitudes | Auggie's activities | what people say
   b. Does it confirm your choice of an adjective in question 1? Why?
   c. What is your favourite moment from the video?

MINI TASK!

You are the writer

Imagine a few lines of the conversation between Summer and August at lunchtime. Why not act it out?

Dans cette leçon, tu as appris :

Vocabulaire p. 68
- Les sentiments
- Les relations

Grammaire p. 71
- Les questions au Prétérit simple

FINAL TASK!

IN GROUPS

Add a passage to the book *Wonder*

Auggie goes on a school trip with his classmates. It is his first sleepaway camp. His parents call him on the second night.

1 Think of the questions Auggie's parents could ask him.

They can be about:

the trip | the place | the weather | the food | the people (classmates, teachers...) | the activities | ....

2 Decide...

- how Auggie is feeling: happy? | VERY happy? | homesick? | excited?
- if he likes... the place | the food | ...
- if his classmates are nice to him.

3 Write his answers accordingly.

- If you decide that Auggie is feeling great:
  - How was your trip?
  - It was great. We had so much fun on the bus!
- If you decide that Auggie is a bit homesick:
  - It was OK, but I miss you, dad...

4 Organize your dialogue just like in a real book.

Regarde à nouveau le dialogue p. 64.

NEED HELP? Follow the guide!

NEED HELP?

Apprends à écrire un dialogue

1 Prends en compte la personnalité des personnages.

Parents

Isabel Pullman	Nate Pullman
worried	*cool*
overprotective	*funny*
loving ...	*supportive ...*

Auggie

brave

...

→ **Quels autres adjectifs te viennent à l'esprit pour décrire la personnalité d'Auggie ?**

2 Pense au contexte.

1re séparation entre Auggie et ses parents

Voyage de fin d'année... Te souviens-tu de l'atmosphère générale en fin d'année dans la bande-annonce ?

excited?

happy?

homesick?

→ **Imagine dans quel état d'esprit se trouve chaque personnage.**

3 Rédige ton dialogue.

- Pense à la ponctuation :

Chaque prise de parole est ponctuée par des **guillemets anglais**.

"She's very pretty," Mom said.
"Yeah, I know," I answered.

La **ponctuation** est à l'intérieur des guillemets.

- Choisis le verbe introducteur qui convient : *say – answer – ask...*

> - Tu peux t'aider de la page 71 de ton manuel pour construire les questions.
> - Inspire-toi du dialogue page 64 si tu as besoin d'aide.

4 Besoin de vocabulaire ? Utilise un dictionnaire bilingue, papier ou en ligne.

WORDS

Apprends ces mots avec leur prononciation !

Feelings

Audio 22nefe5404

joyful

hopeful /əʊ/

proud /aʊ/

ex**ci**ted /ɪk'saɪtɪd/

worried, **ner**vous /ɜː/

petrified = very a**fraid**, **sca**red

an**noyed**, **an**gry, mad at **some**body

Personality

Audio 22nefe5405

kind
friendly
loving
sup**por**tive
com**pa**ssionate
open-**min**ded, **to**lerant
brave = cou**ra**geous
/kə'reɪdʒəs/

mean, **nas**ty
cruel
/'kruːəl/
rude
/ruːd/
narrow-**min**ded, in**to**lerant
/əʊ/ /aɪ/

Relationships

Audio 22nefe5406

be close (to sb),
get on well (with sb)

help, sup**port**

welcome somebody
be friends with sb
make friends with sb

- ac**cept dif**ferences
- be ac**cep**ted
- re**spect** / be re**spec**ted
/rɪ'spekt/ /ɪ/

argue
/'ɑːgjuː/

laugh at somebody
/lɑːf/
= make fun of somebody

bully = **frigh**ten, hurt, or **threa**ten (a smaller or weaker person)

re**ject** / feel re**jec**ted
judge
criticize
/aɪ/

- look down on somebody
- ig**nore** somebody

Les sentiments

1 Chainspeaking!

Répète les mots suivants et ajoute d'autres adjectifs exprimant des sentiments :

proud → worried → ...

Fais la chaîne la plus longue possible (de mémoire, livre fermé !)

Pourquoi ne pas jouer à 2 ?

C'est encore plus amusant !

2 Dictation time! Audio 22nefe5407

Tu vas entendre six adjectifs. Écris-les en faisant bien attention à l'orthographe !

1. worried
2. ...
3. ...
4. ...
5. ...
6. ...

Personnalité – Relations

3 a. **Classe ces verbes selon leur sens : positif ou négatif ?**

make fun of somebody – ignore somebody – make friends with somebody – laugh at somebody – be narrow-minded – be open-minded – look down on somebody

🙂	🙁

b. **Ajoute au moins deux nouveaux verbes dans chaque colonne.**

Si tu en trouves plus de deux, c'est super !

4 **Crée deux nouvelles affiches sur le modèle de celle-ci, en remplaçant les adjectifs entourés.**

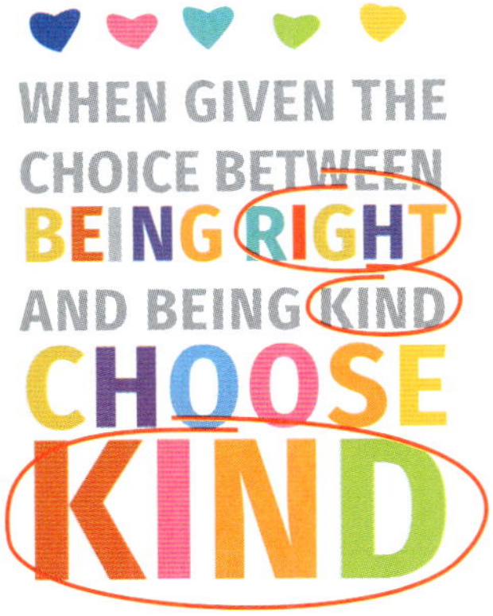

5 **Complète ce paragraphe sur Auggie :**

On his first day at Beecher Prep School, Auggie is ... . He thinks that the other children will ... him because of the way he looks. Indeed, one of the students, Julian, is ... to Auggie. He always ... him. But soon Auggie ... a lot of new friends. One of his first friends is Jack Will. They ... very well. Summer is also very ... to Auggie. She sits with him at lunch and soon they become very ... to each other.

6 Listen up! Audio 22nefe5408

Tu vas entendre quatre phrases incomplètes. Trois mots te seront proposés pour compléter chacune.
Écoute bien et choisis le mot qui convient.

The students in my class are very kind and helpful. They're really...
rude / tolerant / friendly

friendly!

7 **Parle-nous de toi et d'un(e) de tes ami(e)s. Écris quelques lignes pour parler de votre amitié.**

Tu peux t'aider des mots de la liste p. 68 !

8 Prononciation Audio 22nefe5409

a. **Écoute ces mots. Entends-tu la différence de prononciation de la lettre en gras ?**

sm**a**rt - s**a**d
/ɑː/ /æ/

b. **Écoute et entraîne-toi à prononcer les mots suivants :**

smart – nasty – laugh – argue – father

Tous ces mots comportent le son /ɑː/

Les sons /ɑː/ et /æ/

- Une des particularités de l'anglais est d'avoir des sons **longs** et d'autres **courts**.
- Apprends à distinguer le son long /ɑː/ du son court /æ/ : a black car
  /æ/ /ɑː/

La présence des deux points signale que la syllabe est longue.

Poursuis l'entraînement WB p. 41

Le pronom relatif *WHO*

➡ Pour donner des précisions sur une <u>personne</u>, on peut utiliser le pronom relatif *WHO*.

This is <u>Isabelle Pullman</u>, **who** is Auggie's mother.
personne

En anglais, pour donner des précisions sur une <u>chose</u>, on emploie le pronom relatif *WHICH*.

This is <u>the helmet</u> which covers Auggie's head.
chose

En français, *WHO* et *WHICH* se traduisent tous les deux par « qui ».

Les pronoms personnels compléments

➡ Pour désigner des personnes ou des choses, on utilise des pronoms personnels :

Pronom personnel **sujet**

She truly wants the best for **him**.

Pronom personnel **complément**

I sat with **her** at the cafeteria.

me
you
him/her/it
us
you
them

Souviens-toi, on utilise 🙂 :
him pour un garçon / homme
her pour une fille / femme
it pour une chose ou un animal non familier
them pour plusieurs personnes ou choses.

1 ★ **De qui parle-t-on ? Écoute cette conversation et lève le doigt dès que tu entends le pronom relatif *who*. Puis essaie de répéter l'une de ces phrases.** Audio 22nefe5410

2 ★★ **Tu réécris la biographie de l'auteure de *Wonder* ! Relie chaque paire de phrases à l'aide du pronom relatif *who*.**

1. *Wonder* was written by <u>an American writer</u>. <u>She</u> is called R.J. Palacio.
   → *Wonder* was written by an American writer **who** is called R. J. Palacio.
2. One day, R.J. Palacio met <u>a little boy</u>. <u>He</u> had a facial deformity.
3. She decided to write a book about <u>this very special boy</u>. <u>He</u> went to school for the very first time at the age of 10.
4. Today, R.J. Palacio often meets <u>young readers</u>. <u>They</u> are always very enthusiastic about *Wonder*.
5. She has also started "Be kind" campaigns with <u>primary students</u>. <u>They</u> always have plenty of great ideas.

3 ★★★ **Fais deviner l'un de tes personnages préférés (ou détestés !) à tes camarades.**
Pense à utiliser le pronom relatif *who* pour éviter les répétitions !

My character is a young man who...

4 ★ **Devine de qui parle August dans chacune des phrases suivantes.**

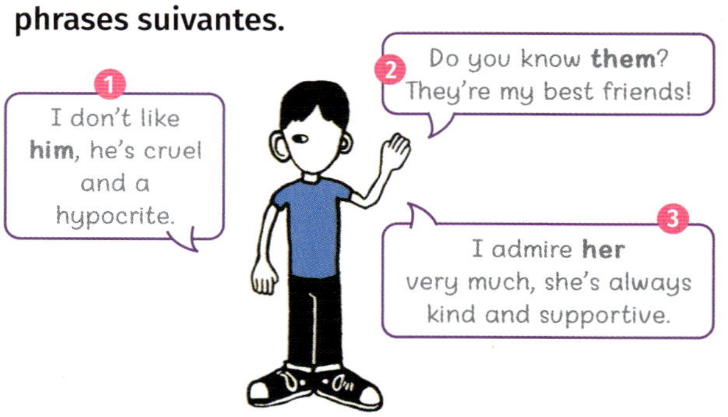

5 ★★ **Réécris les phrases pour éviter les répétitions.**

1. Summer is August's friend, she sits with <u>August</u> at lunch.
2. August has a dog called "Daisy". He likes to play with <u>his dog</u>.
3. Some pupils are mean with August, so he is afraid of <u>these pupils</u>.

Utilise des pronoms personnels compléments à la place des éléments soulignés.

6 ★★ **Réponds au quiz de ton professeur !**

1. Do you know August? / Of course, I know ....
2. Does August have a good relationship with his sister Via? / Yes, he likes ... very much.
3. When does August first meet Jack and Summer? He meets ... on the first day of school.
4. Is August afraid of school at the beginning? / Yes, at first he finds ... quite scary.

LESSON 2

Les questions au Prétérit simple

Pour poser des questions sur des événements passés, on peut utiliser le Prétérit simple.

Sujet ↓ ↓ Base verbale

"**Did** you like your teachers?" Yes, I **did**. / No, I **didn't**.

↑ Auxiliaire *DO* au Prétérit

Pour les questions, les négations et les réponses courtes, on utilise l'auxiliaire ***DO***. C'est lui qui prend la marque du Prétérit : ***did***.

Sujet ↓ ↓ Base verbale

"How **did** you meet Summer?"

↑ Auxiliaire *DO* au Prétérit

Comment poser une question avec *BE* ?

BE étant à la fois verbe et auxiliaire, on inverse le sujet et *BE*.

Sujet ↓

"**Was** Jack with you?"

↑ Auxiliaire *BE* au Prétérit

Sujet ↓

"**Were** they nice?"

↑ Auxiliaire *BE* au Prétérit

On peut commencer une question par un **mot interrogatif** :

Who qui
What que, quoi
How comment
Where où
When quand

→ *Who is August?*

1 ✱ ***Be kind!* Aide un(e) camarade à formuler ces questions en remettant les mots dans l'ordre.**

1. did / see / What / you / ?
2. need / your sister / help / Did / ?
3. of / August / was / afraid / What / ?
4. his / friends / were / Who / ?

Les majuscules te permettront de savoir quel est le premier mot 🙂

2 ✱✱ **Un nouvel élève est arrivé dans ta classe. Quelles questions pourrais-tu lui poser pour qu'il se sente bien accueilli ?**

1. What ... your name? (*be*)
2. Where ... you ... before? (*live*)
3. What school ... you ... to? (*go*)
4. How ... you ... your arm? (*break*)
5. ... it ... ? (*hurt*)

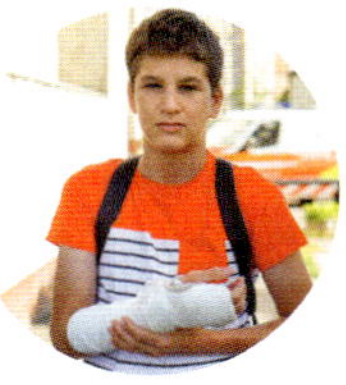

Pense à choisir le bon temps : Présent ou Prétérit.

3 ✱✱✱ **Voyons si tu as une bonne mémoire ! Pense à ton dernier jour en classe de 6e l'an dernier, puis écoute les questions posées et réponds-y. Compare avec tes camarades** 🙂

Audio 22nefe5411

4 Prononciation Audio 22nefe5412

a. Écoute ces questions et répète-les.

1. What did you do in science class?
2. Who sat next to you in class?
3. Why did you cry?

Par quels mots commencent-elles ?

b. Écoute d'autres questions et répète-les. Compare leur intonation avec les précédentes. Remarques-tu une différence ?

4. Did you invite Jack for a sleepover?
5. Were your classmates nice with you?
6. Was Julian nasty again?

L'intonation des questions

- En anglais, l'intonation des **questions ouvertes** (on dit aussi « questions en *WH-* ») est généralement ***descendante*** ↘ :
  Where did you meet Summer? ↘
- L'intonation des **questions fermées** (on peut y répondre par oui ou non) est généralement ***montante*** ↗ :
  Did you make new friends? ↗

Poursuis l'entraînement
WB p. 43

Choose your activities!

Early finishers

Do it yourself!

Create an "I'm unique" poster

- Think about positive or funny things about yourself.
- Create your poster:
  – draw your portrait,
  – add your comments,
  – find a precept that makes you feel good!

Acting time!

Audio 22nefe5413

- Listen to this poem, then read it aloud.
- Think about how to act out each line. Rehearse, then perform for the class!

TELL ME
by Shel Silverstein

Tell me I'm clever,
Tell me I'm kind,
Tell me I'm talented,
Tell me I'm cute,
Tell me I'm sensitive,
Graceful and wise,
Tell me I'm perfect–
But tell me the *truth*.

→ **Challenge:** **now, change the adjectives!**

Class decoration time!

→ **Create a friendship garland to decorate the classroom!**
- Write the name of a classmate on a piece of coloured paper.
- Write down their best quality.
- Link your piece of paper with all the rest to make a paper garland!

Have your say!

Read this post.

Choose Kind @IChooseKind - 22 oct. 2018

Roald Dahl's thoughts on #kindness #choosekind

49 46

→ **What about you? What is your number one quality in a human being?** Why? Write a few lines about it.

a sense of humour

generosity

loyalty

honesty

Did you know about... *Wonder*?

"IF YOU HAVE A CHOICE BETWEEN BEING RIGHT AND BEING KIND, CHOOSE KIND."

Since its publication in 2012, *Wonder* has become a favorite of teenagers and educators all over the USA. It has been published in 45 countries, and has sold over 5 million copies worldwide.

The book has inspired the Choose Kind movement, an anti-bullying campaign designed to encourage students, educators, families, and readers of all ages to combat bullying by practicing everyday acts of kindness.

A QUESTION TO THE AUTHOR

Why is the book called *Wonder*?

"Natalie Merchant has an amazing song called *Wonder*, and the joyfulness and optimism of that song—not to mention the theme of being born "different"—really helped me shape my vision of the book."

R.J. Palacio

→ **Why not listen to this song?** Video 22nefe5414

READING CORNER

Previously in *FENCE* ...

Nicholas has met the other competitors. It is now time to confront his biggest rival...

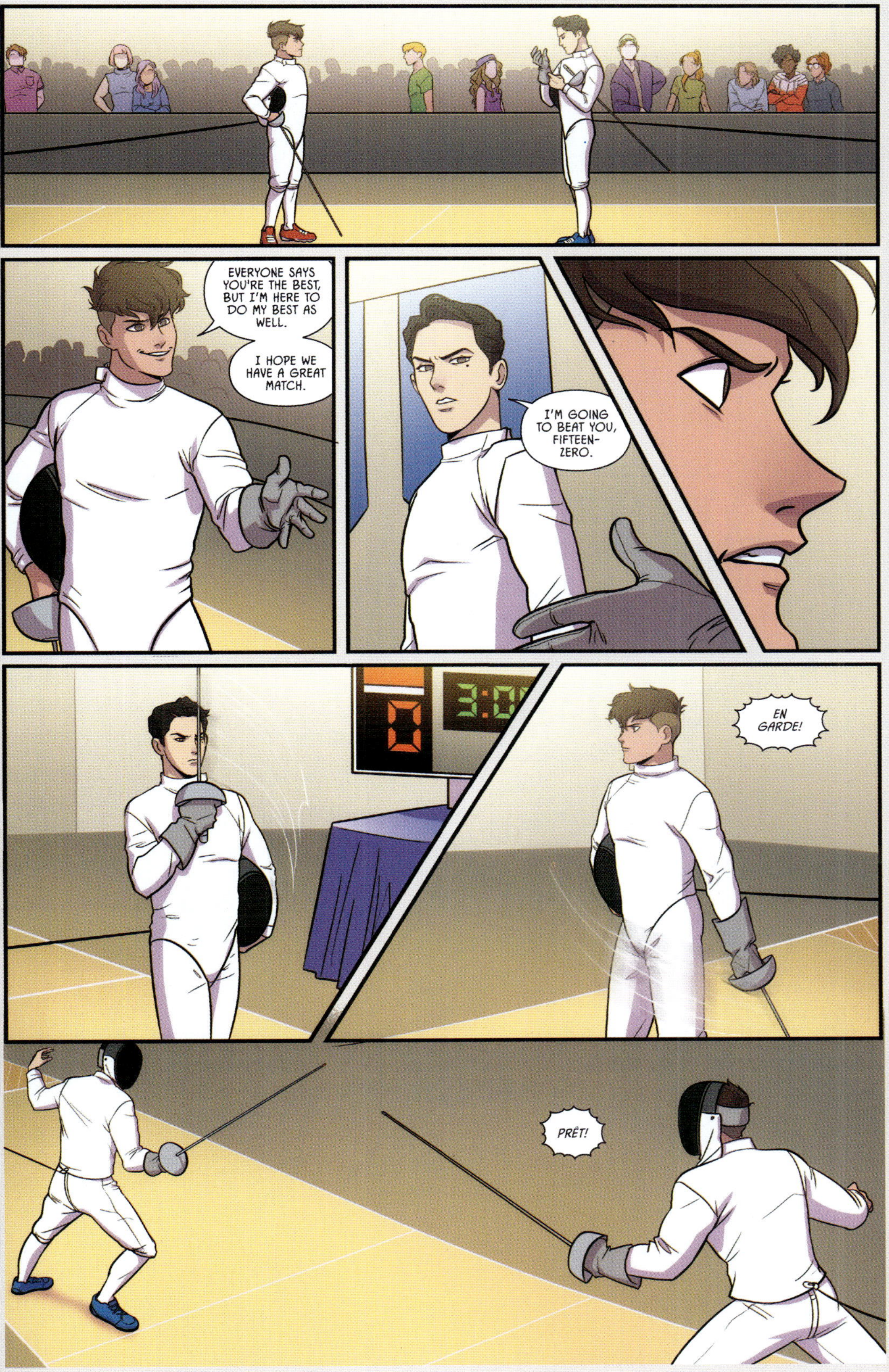

1. overseas = *à l'étranger*
2. a scholarship = *une bourse*

HELP

- Ces pages te permettent enfin de découvrir Seiji. Pour apprendre qui il est, concentre-toi sur :
  - *sa posture*
  - *les expressions de son visage*
  - *ce qu'il dit à Nicholas*
  - *ce que les autres disent de lui.*
- Les bulles «éclairs» (PRÊT!) sont les instructions prononcées par l'arbitre. Tu as remarqué une chose amusante ? 😊

PICK AN ACTIVITY

- **Imagine** why Seiji went to France.
- **Act out** the meeting between Nicholas and Seiji. *→ vignettes 8 & 9.*

Think about each character's emotions.

- **Imagine** how the duel will go. Place your bets about the winner!

To be continued on p. 84

TRAPPED in HAMPTON COURT!

PLAY IN TEAMS

ESCAPE GAME

The six portraits of King Henry VIII's wives are missing from the palace.
Find them or the ghosts of Henry's wives won't let you out!

Au cours de cet *escape game*, vous allez :

- Découvrir le palais de Hampton Court, un lieu incroyable où l'horreur et le faste se côtoient !
- Résoudre des énigmes et surmonter des obstacles… Parviendrez-vous à vous échapper ?

Vocabulaire
- Royauté
- *Escape game*
- Dire les dates

Grammaire **Révisions**
- Le Prétérit
- Les dates

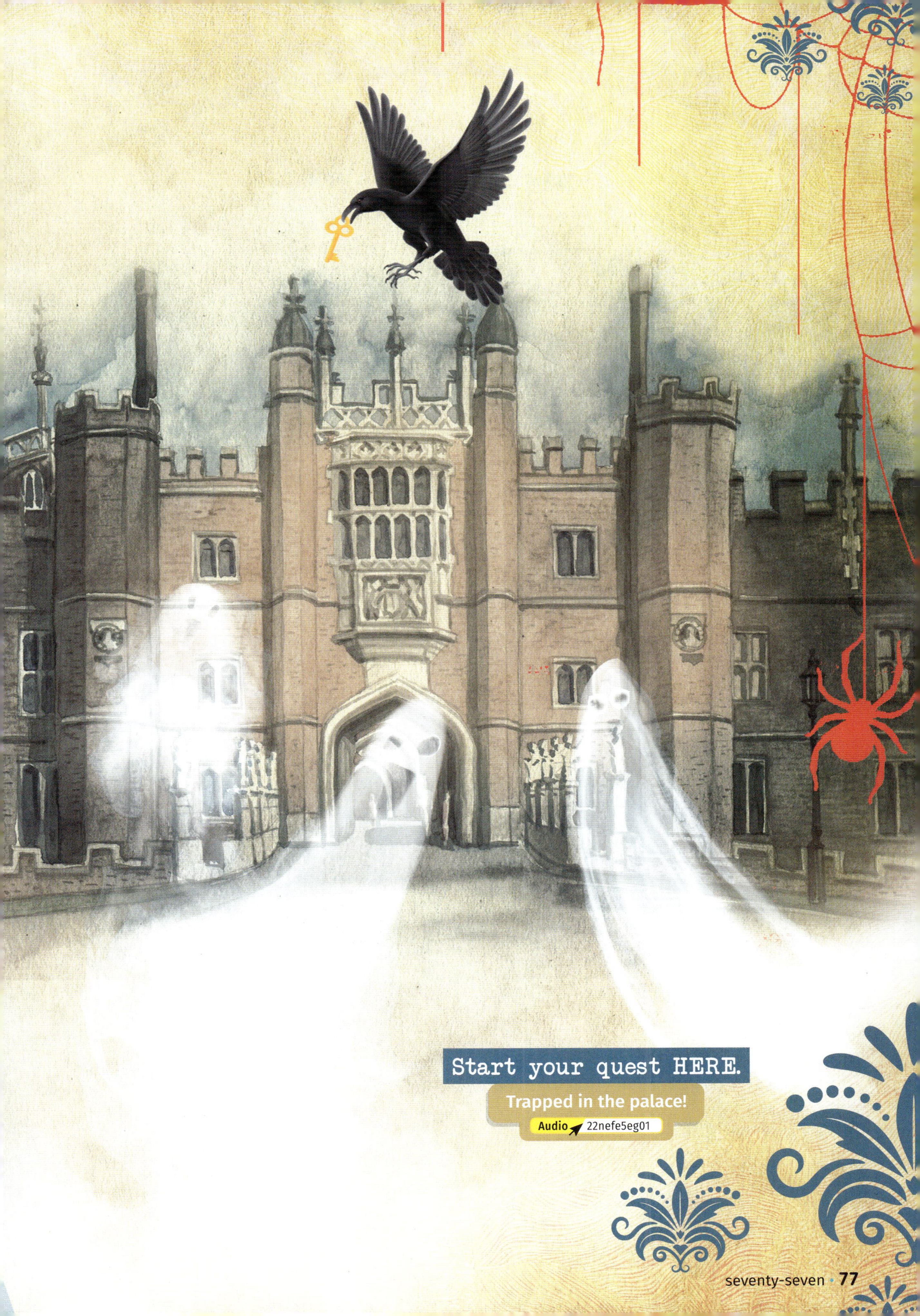

Start your quest HERE.

Trapped in the palace!

Audio 22nefe5eg01

IN THE KING'S CHAMBERS

Henry VIII's most famous residence, Hampton Court Palace, near London, was devoted to pleasure and festivity. Around 1540, Hampton Court was the most modern, sophisticated and magnificent palace in England. Watch the video and discover the place!

Welcome to Hampton Court Palace

Video 22nefe5eg02

PLAY IN TEAMS

YOUR MISSION

You are in the King's chambers. Several challenges await you. After each challenge, go and see the guard. If you succeed, he will give you one of the missing portraits.

1 Henry VIII was born in Greenwich, London, on 28th June, 1491.

2 He was crowned King in 1509. He reigned for thirty-eight years.

3 He had six successive wives and three children.

4 Henry VIII was really tall at 6 foot 2 inches (= 1 m 88)

5 He ruled in the Tudor period.

6 Hampton Court Palace was one of Henry's homes.

The Tudor dynasty ruled England from 1485 to 1603.
There were five Tudor monarchs: **Henry VII** (ruled 1485–1509), **Henry VIII** (ruled 1509–47), **Edward VI** (ruled 1547–53), **Mary I** (ruled 1553–58), and **Elizabeth I** (ruled 1558–1603).
During the Tudor period, the monarch was the most powerful person in the land.

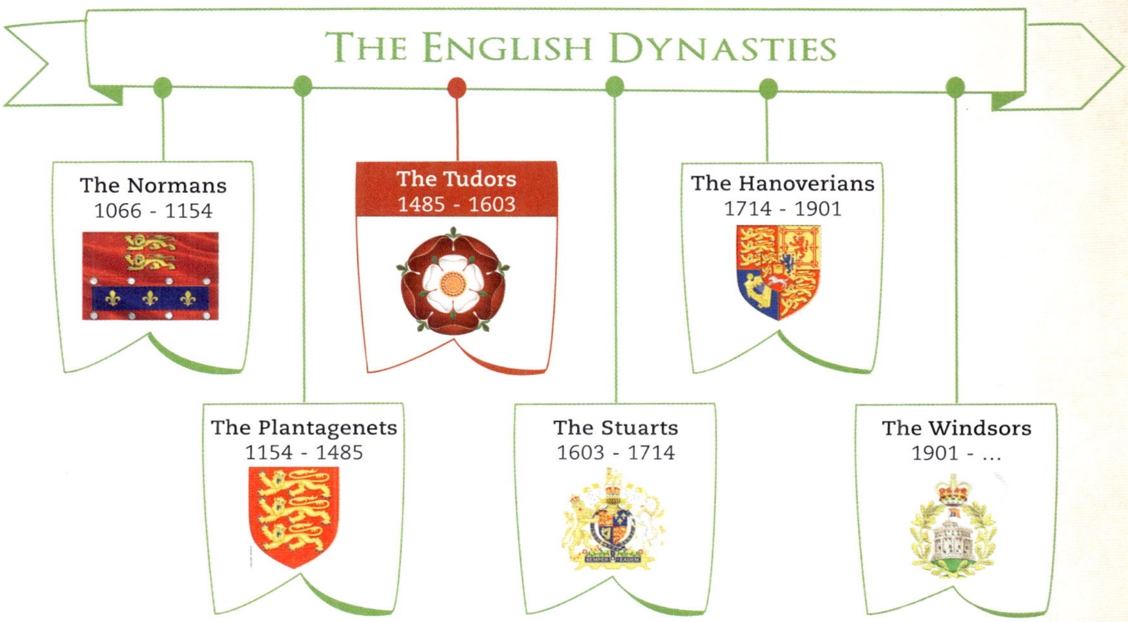

7 Henry VIII was quite cruel and temperamental... He had many people executed because he considered them as traitors.

8 Henry VIII broke away from the Catholic church and created his own church: the Church of England.

9 Henry VIII loved sports. He was very athletic.

10 Henry died on 28th January, 1547 at the age of 55.

CHALLENGE 1 Memorise as much information as you can about Henry VIII and answer a quiz about him. WB p. 47

CHALLENGE 2 Watch a video about sports at Hampton Court and crack the code. WB p. 48

Sports at Hampton Court Palace
Video 22nefe5eg03

CHALLENGE 3 Listen to an audio guide and complete Henry's family tree. WB p. 49

Audio guide about Henry VIII's family
Audio 22nefe5eg04

Henry VIII's wives

Got the three portraits? Well done! Now move on to other parts of the palace to find the three other missing portraits.

ALL OVER

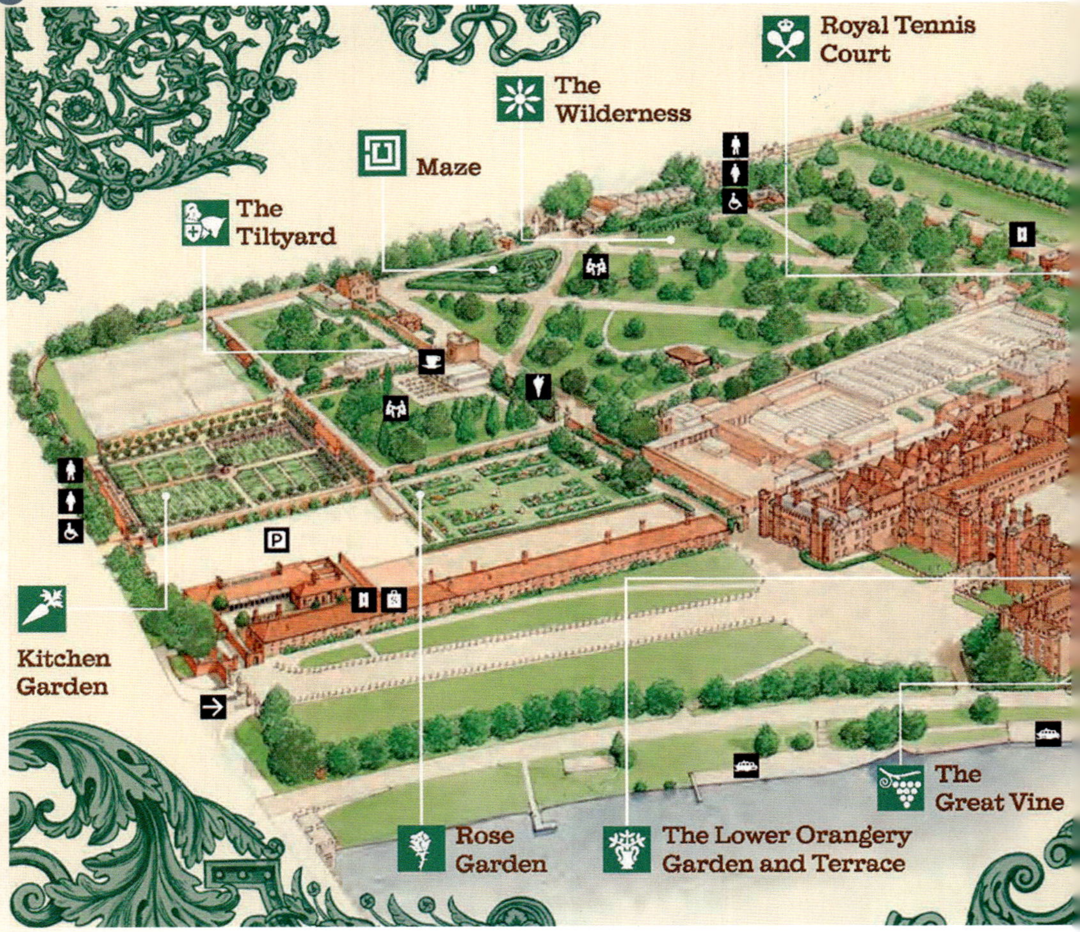

PLAY IN TEAMS

YOUR MISSION

Your search for the three portraits continues. In each area of the palace you visit, a challenge awaits you!

CHALLENGE 4

The fourth portrait is locked in the maze. Listen to the gardener's instructions to find it. WB p. 50

The Maze
Audio 22nefe5eg05

CHALLENGE 5

Here you are in the Great Dining Hall! The cook will help you get portrait n°5 if you give him the password WB p. 51

THE CASTLE

" It is the most famous maze in the history of the world, and immeasurably the one most visited. "
Ernest Law, 1926

CHALLENGE 6

Listen to a song and find out what happened to Henry's wives. WB p. 52

The song Video 22nefe5eg06

Once you have collected all the portraits, complete your portrait gallery with the fate of the six wives. WB p. 46

FINAL CHALLENGE

Have you found all the portraits? Congratulations! Now one final challenge awaits you! Listen to the ghosts' last request... If you can answer their question, you'll be free at last!

Final challenge Audio 22nefe5eg07

WORDS

Apprends ces mots avec leur prononciation !

Life at the palace

Audio 22nefe5eg08

a **mon**arch
the king
the queen

be crowned
/aʊ/
rule = **gov**ern

a **ban**quet
/'bæŋkwɪt/

a spoon
a plate
a glass
a knife
a fork

Henry VIII

- **cru**el, tempera**men**tal, **jea**lous
  /'kruːəl/ /'dʒeləs/
- a fate = a **des**tiny
- a wife / wi**v**es
  /aɪ/
- **mar**ry
- di**vorce**
- **ex**ecute
  /juː/

Escape game

Audio 22nefe5eg09

a clue = an indi**ca**tion, a tip
/uː/
a **chal**lenge
solve a **ri**ddle / a **mys**tery
find the **pass**word
crack / break a code

es**ca**pe from a maze = es**ca**pe from a **la**byrinth
/ɪ/

Directions

Audio 22nefe5eg10

go straight on

go across

turn left / turn right

La vie à la Cour

1 ✱ **Trouve l'intrus et remplace-le par un mot qui convient.**

1. monarch – queen – wife – prince
2. mean – temperamental – kind – jealous
3. fork – violin – knife – spoon

Indiquer la direction

2 ✱✱✱ **Guide ton voisin jusqu'à un repère : saura-t-il le trouver ? Prépare l'itinéraire dans ton cahier puis dicte-le lui !**

Turn left, then go straight on…

Les dates et les nombres

→ p. 83

3 ✱ IN PAIRS **Note quatre années dans ton cahier. Dicte-les à ton voisin : saura-t-il les écrire correctement ?**

fifteen o-nine

1509

4 Dictation time! Audio 22nefe5eg11

✱ **Tu vas entendre le nom de membres de la famille Tudor. Complète chaque nom avec le numéro de règne que tu entends :**

Elizabeth … Henry … Edward …
Henry … Mary …

5 ✱✱ **Utilise le vocabulaire de la famille pour présenter l'arbre généalogique de Henry VIII. Note 8 phrases dans ton cahier. Aide-toi de l'arbre complété au challenge 3 !**

Elizabeth I is Henry VIII's daughter.

Le Prétérit simple

Révisions → p. 55 et 71

Henry VIII **loved** sports.
He **met** Anne de Cleves in 1540.

Verbes réguliers → terminaison *-ed*
Verbes irréguliers → liste p. 158

Where **did** he live?
He **didn't** agree with the Catholic Pope.

Pour les questions, les négations et les réponses courtes, on utilise l'auxiliaire ***DO***. C'est lui qui prend la marque du Prétérit : *did*.

Dates & numbers

Audio 22nefe5eg14

On écrit :	On dit :
1491	fourteen ninety-one
1509	fifteen o-nine
1547	fifteen forty-seven

On écrit :	On dit :
Henry VII	Henry the seventh
Henry VIII	Henry the eighth
Elizabeth I	Elizabeth the first

1 Dictation time!

Audio 22nefe5eg12

Écoute et complète ces phrases.

1. Henry VIII ... six women.
2. He ... two of his wives.
3. Three others ....
4. Only one wife ..., she was lucky!

2 Le panneau explicatif de la vie de Henry VIII a été endommagé. Rédige les légendes qui ont disparu en utilisant ces verbes :

become king | create | be born | rule | be | have

Attention, certains verbes sont irréguliers. → Liste p. 158

1. ....

2. ....

3. ....

4. ....

5. He ruled in The Tudor period.

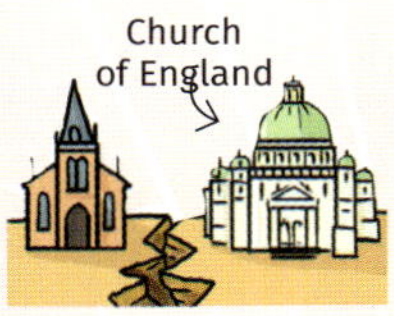

6. ....

3 Listen up!

Audio 22nefe5eg13

Tu vas entendre quatre phrases qui contiennent chacune une date. Écoute bien et complète-les ci-dessous.

1. Henry VIII married Catherine of Aragon in ...
2. They divorced in ...
3. Anne Boleyn was executed in ...
4. Henry VIII married his last wife in ...

4 *Questions for a champion!*

Réponds à ces questions.

	Points
What nationality was Henry VIII?	100
How many women did he marry?	100
Where did they live?	200
What sports did he like to play? (x3)	200
Total	...

Make complete sentences and count your points!

READING CORNER

Previously in *FENCE* **...**

The game opposing Nicholas to Seiji is on. Who will win?

1. rookie = *débutant*
2. a touch = *une touche, qui peut donner un point*
3. rattle = *ici, réussir à toucher l'épée de l'adversaire*
4. a southpaw = a left hander

To be continued on p. 100

HELP

- Pour savoir comment se déroule le match, regarde bien :
  – *les trois première vignettes,*
  – *ce que se dit Nicholas tout au long du duel.*
  À ton avis, qui gagne pour le moment ?
- Les pensées de Nicholas permettent de comprendre sa personnalité. Comment le décrirais-tu ?
- Les bulles « éclair » sont dites par l'arbitre (*the referee*). Comme il est anglophone, comment penses-tu qu'il prononce ces mots ?

PICK AN ACTIVITY

Imagine Seiji's thoughts during the match and draw thought bubbles in your copybook.

Act out the duel!

Seiji | Nicholas | the referee

Who will win? Place your bets!

PROJECT

5

Dinner and a movie

Dans ce chapitre, tu vas :

- Découvrir des cinémas américains très originaux
- Apprendre à acheter une place de cinéma et à commander de la nourriture

Vocabulaire

- Au cinéma
- Au restaurant

Grammaire

- *Want to, would like to*
- Les déterminants *a(n)*, *ø*

JEU NUMÉRIQUE

Prepare food orders!

Are you ready for a typically American experience? Get comfortable and enjoy!

First, take a tour of an amazing dine-in movie theatre in the US!

Video 22nefe5501

LESSON 1

Pick your movie

1 What film do you want to see?

1. **Look at these posters.** Do you know any of these movies?
2. **Listen to Mai-Linh and Emile.** Audio 22nefe5502
   Can you identify the film they want to see?
3. **What about the other movies?**
   Do you remember what they are about? WB p. 53

Time to write Text a friend to say which of these movies you would like to see. WB p. 53

Fun Fact!

Films are released on Fridays in the USA and on Wednesdays in France. So sometimes, the French are the first to discover international blockbusters!

WEDNESDAY FRIDAY

2 When do you want to see it?

1 Look at this booking screen of a dine-in theatre website. Spot:

- ✔ the title of the movie
- ✔ the location of the theatre
- ✔ the dates and times of the screening
- ✔ the price
- ✔ the seats
- ✔ the rating

WB p. 54

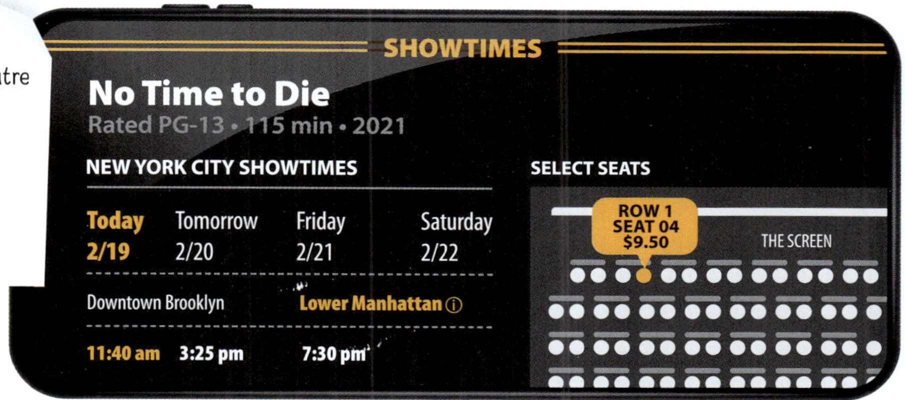

Alamo Drafthouse booking screen

i

Money

1 dollar ~ 0,84 euro.

→ How much does a ticket cost in euros?

Time & date

- Look at the way people write the date in the USA:

Friday **2/21**

→ What do you notice?

- Look at the time:

11:40 am **3:25 pm**

→ Do you know what "am" and "pm" mean?

2 Listen to Mai-Linh and Emile book their tickets. Audio 22nefe5503

a. Label the screenshot in your workbook. WB p. 54

b. Colour in their reservation details. WB p. 54

MINI TASK

Book your ticket

What would you like to see?

1. Go to the Alamo website* and choose:

your theatre | your movie | the date and time | your seat

2. Book your ticket 🙂. WB p. 54

3. Get ready to share what you would like to see with your classmates.

I would like to see *Captain America* because...

*drafthouse.com

Dans cette leçon, tu as appris :

Vocabulaire ▶▶ p. 94
- Au cinéma

Grammaire ▶▶ p. 96
- *Want to / would like to*

Révisions
- Le pronom relatif *who*

LESSON 2

Order your food

A

B

C

D

E

F

KIDS

CHOOSE YOUR OWN ADVENTURE! **$ 7**
Choose one main dish, side item and a sweet

CHOOSE ONE MAIN DISH

- ☐ **Turkey Meatball Mini-Burgers (2)** with a Side of Honey Mustard
- ☐ **Baked Ham & Cheese Sandwich** with Honey Ham, Green Apple & a Side of Honey Mustard
- ☐ **Quesadilla*** with Sweet Potato, Black Beans, Mozzarella & Spinach
- ☐ **Chicken Strips (2)** with a Side of Honey Mustard

CHOOSE ONE SIDE

- ☐ Apple sauce*
- ☐ Roasted Broccoli with Parmesan*
- ☐ Carrots & Hummus*
- ☐ Yogurt with Honey & Strawberries*
- ☐ French Fries with Ketchup*

CHOOSE ONE SWEET

- ☐ Chocolate Chip Cookie*
- ☐ Peanut Butter Banana Cookie*
- ☐ M&M'S*
- ☐ Sour Patch Kids*

** vegetarian items*

Menu or "A la carte"?

1 **Look at the menu.**
a. Name the five different parts.
b. Work on words to understand the menu. WB p. 55

2 **Match the menu and the pictures.**

> Picture (C) is mozzarella sticks!

HELP

Dans un nom composé, le mot principal est en dernière position 🙂.
"tomato sauce"

3 **Listen to Mai-Linh and Emile.** Audio 22nefe5504
a. Take their orders. WB p. 56
b. Practise playing waiter Audio 22nefe5505 or customer. Audio 22nefe5506

Time to write Label more American food. WB p. 57

Food from around the world

The USA is very multicultural, so the food is too! Check the menu and find:

Mexican food | Italian food | Middle Eastern Food | ...

Drinks

1 oz = 1 ounce ≈ 3 cl
→ How much do you get if you order a 12-oz drink?

MENU

A LA CARTE

- ☐ **Cheese Pizza*** $6
  Tomato sauce & Mozzarella - Add Pepperoni, Sausage or Mushrooms - $ 1 Each
- ☐ **Chicken & Broccoli Pasta Bake** $7
  Tomatoes, Basil Pesto, Mozzarella & Parmesan
- ☐ **Egg-in-a-Hole** $6
  Bacon, Cheese, Toast & a Side of Fruit
- ☐ **Mozzarella Sticks (5)*** $6
  Tomato sauce
- ☐ **Kid's Popcorn*** $3
  Butter Upon Request, No Free Refills

DRINKS & SHAKES

ALL SERVED IN A SOUVENIR CUP

- ☐ **Drinks (12 oz)** $2
  Glass of Milk, Soda, Orange Juice or Organic Apple Juice
- ☐ **Milkshake** $3
  Chocolate, Vanilla, Strawberry, or Cookie
- ☐ **Strawberry Banana Smoothie** $4
  Strawberry Banana puree, Greek Yogurt, Fresh Orange Juice
- ☐ **Blueberry Pancake Shake** $4
  Vanilla Ice Cream, Fresh Blueberries, Maple Syrup

Alamo Drafthouse Kids menu

MINI TASK!

Place your order IN PAIRS

1. **Choose your role:**
   customer | waiter
2. **Act out the scene!**
   - *Customer:* Place your order and prepare your money.
   - *Waiter:* Interact with the customer and take the order.

> Would you like a dessert?

Dans cette leçon, tu as appris :

Vocabulaire » p. 94
- Au restaurant

Grammaire » p. 97
- Les déterminants *a, an, ø*

Révisions
- Les noms composés

FINAL TASK!

IN GROUPS

Organise an evening at your own dine-in movie theatre!

Pense à utiliser le lexique p. 94.

1 Create your movie program.

Choose three films you want to screen and design your program:

film posters | dates | times | price | seating chart

Fiche 22nefe5519

2 Prepare the menu.

food | drinks | prices

Choose your type of cuisine:

Italian? | fast-food? | veggie? | Asian? | ...

Fiche 22nefe5520

3 Share your "Dinner and a movie" program with the other groups.

4 Let the show begin!

Tell the waiter what you would like to see, eat and drink.

- Sell the movie ticket.
- Take the food order.

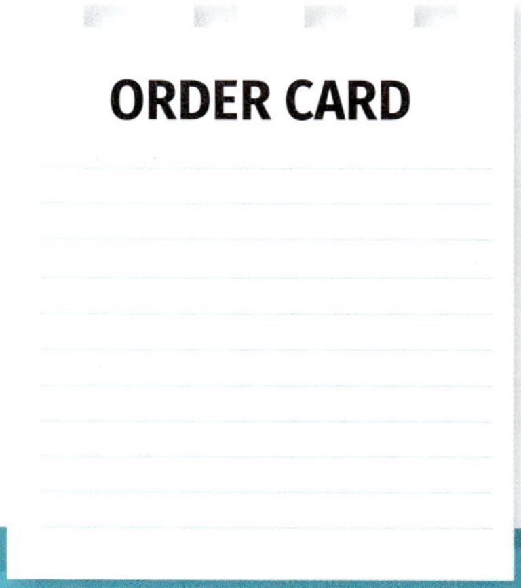

NEED HELP? Follow the guide!

NEED HELP?

Entraîne-toi à poser des questions et à y répondre

1 Choisis ton film !

a. Écoute ce premier échange. Entraîne-toi à le répéter. Audio 22nefe5507

What would you like to see?

I really want to see *Night at the Museum*. It sounds great!

b. À toi de jouer ! Entraîne-toi avec un ou une camarade en choisissant un autre film. Puis échangez les rôles.

2 Ensuite, la séance !

a. Écoute et entraîne-toi à répéter.

What day do you want to go on?

I'd like to go **on** Tuesday **at eleven thirty am.**

b. À vous de jouer ! Entraînez-vous en choisissant d'autres séances.

Monday – 4.15 pm

Wednesday – 10.30 am

Saturday – 7.45 pm

3 Puis, le menu !

a. Écoute et entraîne-toi à répéter.

What would you like to eat?
What can I get you?

Er… **I'll have** two chicken strips with French fries, please. **How much** is it?

b. À vous de jouer ! Entraînez-vous en choisissant d'autres plats dans le menu p. 90-91.

4 Pour finir, il faut payer…

a. Écoute et entraîne-toi à répéter.

That's 10 dollars, please! **How** would you like to pay? Cash or credit card?

OK, cash please. Here you go.

b. À vous de jouer ! Entraînez-vous en choisissant d'autres prix.

Si tu ne comprends pas, n'hésite pas à le dire :
"Sorry, I missed what you said! Can you repeat please?"

WORDS

Apprends ces mots avec leur prononciation !

At the cinema

Audio 22nefe5508

"What time is the **mov**ie?"
"The **mov**ie is at 6.15" / "There's a **scree**ning at 6.15." (six fifteen)

a **com**edy
a **dra**ma /ˈdrɑmə/
a ro**man**tic **com**edy
an **an**imated **mov**ie /eɪ/ /ˈmuvi/
an **ac**tion film
a **fan**tasy film /s/
a **hor**ror film /ˈhɒrər/

a **mo**vie **the**atre = a **ci**nema
go to the **ci**nema / go to the **mov**ies
buy a **ti**cket / book a **ti**cket /ɪ/
choose your seat

the screen

a row = a line of seats /rəʊ/

a**vai**lable = free /əˈveɪləbəl/

funny ≠ sad

scary **mov**ing

boring ≠ enter**tai**ning

Food

Audio 22nefe5509

turkey /ˈtɜːki/

ham

bacon and eggs

chicken

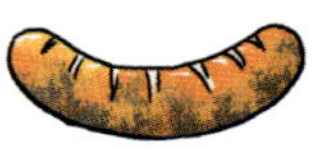
a **sau**sage /ˈsɒsɪdʒ/

meatballs /iː/

cheese /iː/

a to**ma**to (*pl. tomatoes*)

a po**ta**to (*pl. potatoes*)

a **sa**lad

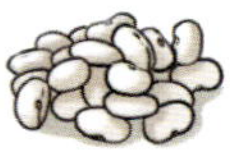
beans /iː/

spinach /ɪtʃ/

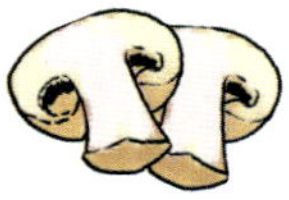
mushrooms

an **ap**ple

a ba**na**na

strawberries

blueberries

a glass of or**ga**nic **ap**ple juice

a **so**da

a va**nil**la **milk**shake

At the restaurant

Audio 22nefe5510

read the **me**nu /ˈmenju/

It looks **tas**ty, de**li**cious /eɪ/

choose a main dish, a side, a sweet/a de**ssert** and a drink
/ɪ/ /aɪ/ /ɪː/ /dɪˈzɜːt/

order your food

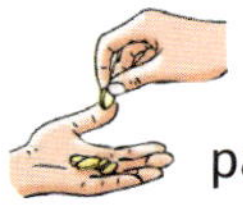
pay

a **quar**ter = 25 cents (25 ¢) /ˈkwɔrtər/

a **dol**lar = 100 cents

"How much is the peanut butter cookie, please?"
"It's three dollars and fifteen cents." ($ 3.15)

Au cinéma

1 **a.** **Associe un genre cinématographique et un adjectif à chaque affiche de film.**

b. **Donne ton avis sur l'un de ces films :**

I really like / I don't like *Minions* because. . .

2 **Associe chaque étiquette au prix correspondant.**

1. twenty twenty-five
2. twelve dollars and twenty-five cents
3. fifteen dollars and three cents
4. fifty seventy-five

3 **Une soirée au cinéma ! Complète ces phrases à l'aide du vocabulaire p. 94.**

1. "Let's ... our tickets for *The Batman*!"
2. "There are three seats available in the second ..." / "Yeah, but I don't want to sit so close to the ..."
3. "There's a special ... of *The Lego Movie* at 9 pm. Shall we go?"

4 **Prononciation** Audio 22nefe5511

a. **Écoute ces paires de nombres et répète-les.**

40 - 14 13 – 30 50 – 15

b. **Écoute et entraîne-toi à prononcer ces phrases.**

Hurry up! The movie starts at 3.15.

Here's your bill. That'll be $14.50.

What's your seat number?

16

L'accentuation des chiffres

- Les nombres de 13 à 19 sont accentués sur la 2e syllabe : thir**teen**
- Les nombres des dizaines (30, 40, 50, 60..) sont accentués sur la 1re syllabe : **thir**ty

Au restaurant

5 **Trouve l'intrus dans chaque série et remplace-le par le mot approprié.**

1. strawberries – banana – sausage – apple
2. meatballs – tomato – chicken – ham
3. cheese – potato – beans – spinach
4. orange juice – strawberry juice – soda – banana juice

6 **Dictation time!** Audio 22nefe5512

Pas facile d'être serveur ! Pour ne rien oublier, écris ce que commande ton client.

7 **Miam, tu vas te régaler !**

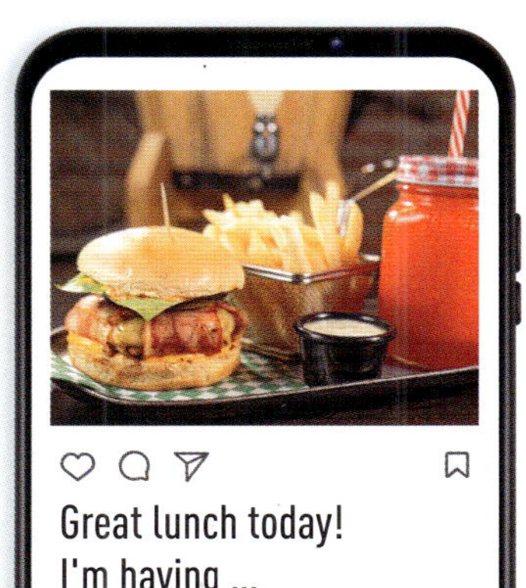

Écris un message pour accompagner la photo de ton repas.

Poursuis l'entraînement WB p. 58

GRAMMAR

LESSON 1

Want / Would like

➡ Pour dire ce que l'on veut ou ce que l'on aimerait, on peut utiliser *want* ou *would like*.

I would like two tickets (N) for "the Lego Movie" please. I don't want front row seats (N).

My father wants to see (to + V) a comedy, but my sister would like to see (to + V) an action film.

L'auxiliaire modal *would* ne change pas, quel que soit le sujet.

Ces deux verbes peuvent être suivis d'un **nom** (ce qu'on veut obtenir) ou d'un **verbe** (ce qu'on aimerait faire).

À l'oral :

- ***would*** est souvent contracté.
  I'd like two tickets please.
- La particule ***to*** est réduite.
  I want to see a comedy.
  /tə/
  → *I wanna see a comedy.*

Question Time

What **do** you want to see? Where **would** you like to sit?

1 ★ **Ton petit frère va au cinéma pour la première fois. Complète ce qu'il dit à l'aide de *want* ou *want to*.**

1. Mum, do you ... popcorn? I do!
2. I ... see the new *Spider-Man* movie!
3. I don't ... a booster seat, I'm big enough!
4. I ... sit near Dad!

2 ★★ **C'est le week-end, dis quelles activités tu aimerais faire... ou pas, à l'aide de "*I would like to*" et "*I don't want to*".**

1 

2 

3 

4 

3 ★★★ **Tes parents essaient de motiver ta petite sœur. D'après ses réponses, retrouve les questions qu'ils lui ont posées.**

1. Do you want to ...? – No, I don't want to go out, it's raining.
2. ...? – Oh no, the supermarket is boring!
3. ...? – Yes, let's watch a TV series. That's a good idea!
4. ...? – Oh yes, I'd love quesadillas for dinner!

4 **Prononciation** Audio 22nefe5513

a. **Regarde et écoute ces mots, puis répète-les.**

would talk walk calm half

b. **Écoute et entraîne-toi à prononcer ces phrases.**

1. Would you like more water?
2. What are you talking about?
3. Keep calm and walk on.

Lettres muettes : le « L » de *would*
Dans l'auxiliaire *would*, comme dans d'autres mots, le « L » est muet.

5 **Le pronom relatif *who*** Révisions → p. 70

antécédent humain

"It's an action movie about a spy **who** goes on dangerous missions... "

★★★ **a.** **Quels films as-tu vus récemment ? Raconte l'histoire en une phrase.**

It's the story of a boy **who**...

b. **Lis les phrases à un camarade. Saura-t-il identifier ces films ?**

LESSON 2

Les déterminants indéfinis : *a(n)*, Ø

Pour désigner des noms dénombrables (*que l'on peut compter*), on utilise :

- ***a* ou *an* avec un nom singulier :**

  It is served in a souvenir cup.

  Can I have an apple crumble?

  Son voyelle

- **Ø avec un nom pluriel :**

  ... with Ø black beans and Ø potatoes.

Pour désigner des noms indénombrables (*que l'on ne peut pas compter*), on utilise Ø :

... with Ø butter and Ø garlic.

1 Rédige quelques phrases pour dire ce que tu aimerais pour le petit déjeuner.

Inclus un plat qui n'est pas sur la carte. Tes camarades pourront-ils l'identifier ?

BREAKFAST ALL DAY
Served with toast

CEREAL
- Oatmeal
- Chocos
- Corn Flakes

BEVERAGES
- Coffee
- Tea
- Milk

FAVORITES
- ESC – *Egg, sausage and cheese*
- French toast
- Pancakes
- Waffles

EGGS
- Veggie omelet – *Onions, green peppers and tomatoes*
- Sunny Side Up – *Eggs fried on only one side*

ON THE SIDE
fresh strawberries – yogurt with fresh fruit – granola

Prépare ce petit déjeuner pour ta famille le week-end prochain. Pense à le prendre en photo avant qu'il ne soit dévoré !

2 Prépare-toi à passer commande ! Complète les phrases avec *a*, *an*, ou Ø.

1. Can I have ... glass of milk, please?
2. I'll have ... pancakes with ... maple syrup, please.
3. I don't like ... jam, I prefer ... honey.
4. I'd like ... almond cookie with ... vanilla milkshake, please.

3 Food art!

a. Décris la composition de ces plats.

To make these owls, you need...
To make this funny face, you need...

1

2

b. Crée ta propre composition à la maison, prends-la en photo et présente-la à la classe !

4 Les noms composés

Révisions → p. 54

honey mustard

Le nom principal apparaît toujours en dernier. Le ou les noms qui le précèdent apportent des précisions à ce nom.

Pour composer ton menu, forme des mots composés à partir des mots suivants :

turkey | meat | strawberry | peanut butter | milkshake | juice | smoothie | sandwich

Combien de plats as-tu inventés ?
Lesquels semblent les plus appétissants ?
... Les moins appétissants ?

Poursuis l'entraînement
WB p. 60

Choose your activities!

Early finishers

Weird but true

Here are some quirky American food habits... Can you guess what food it is?

1 

a. vanilla and chocolate donuts?

b. deep-fried oreos?

2 

a. spray cheese?

b. mashed carrots?

3 

a. hot dogs?

b. corn dogs?

Which one would you like to taste?

Which food is really weird?

→ **In your opinion, what French food habits would be weird for Americans?**

Create your own "quirky French food habits" and illustrate it.

Personality Test

Tell me what you eat, I'll tell you who you are!

1 First, what do you want for breakfast?

a. Pancakes ✶

b. Toast ♣

c. Eggs and Bacon ■

d. Cereal ♦

Did you know about...

In the 50s, there were over 5,000 Drive-In Theatres all across the USA.

2 What would you like for lunch?

a. Poached salmon and wild rice ♣
b. Ramen noodles ♦
c. Quesadilla ■
d. Burger and fries ✶

3 Where do you put your ketchup?

a. On the side of the plate ✶
b. All over the food ♦
c. In a separate dish ■
d. Ew! No ketchup! ♣

4 Choose your dessert:

a. Pear crumble ♦
b. Apple sauce ✶
c. Fresh fruit salad ♣
d. Cheesecake ■

5 What is your most important rule?

a. I'm a vegetarian ♣
b. Different foods should never mix ✶
c. There is no rule! ■
d. I don't eat salad ♦

6 And finally, which drink will go best with these meals?

a. Water ♣
b. Soda ■
c. Apple juice ♦
d. Hot chocolate ✶

♣ You're a healthy, reasonable person who enjoys a nice meal. You're always very careful with what you eat. – ■ You're a spontaneous person who loves eating comfort food. – ♦ You're an energetic person who likes eating healthy food even if a little junk food is OK from time to time!! – ✶ You're a connoisseur. You know what good food is...

*pretty (*adv*) = *assez*

Fun Fact!

In July 2021, the Alamo Drafthouse screened Jaws on the water, in Austin, Texas! → Can you imagine why? Would you go?

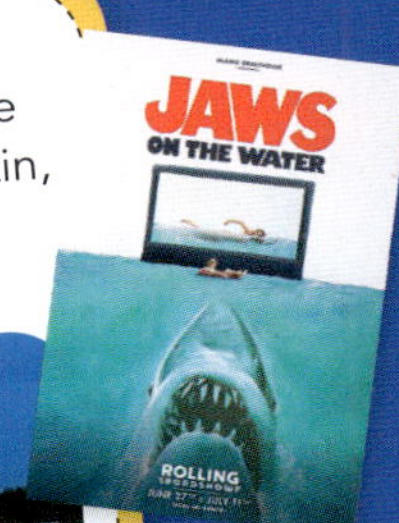

Drive-in theatres ?

Today, there are about 325 Drive-in Movie Theatres in the United States.

→ **Think of a new type of movie theatre.**
Suggest a movie and an amazing place to watch it!

Let's riddle!

→ If you go to the movies and you're paying, is it cheaper to take one friend to the movies twice*, or two friends to the movies at the same time?

* *deux fois*

READING CORNER

Previously in *FENCE*...

Nicholas and Seiji had their first duel. Now it is time for the score...

1. "he's not in my bracket" = *"il n'est pas dans ma poule"*
2. Exton = a prestigious fencing school

HELP

- Tu veux connaître le score ? Essaie de repérer des chiffres dans le texte des bulles. 😊
- Concentre-toi sur les vignettes qui montrent Nicholas. Observe sa posture, l'expression de son visage, l'aspect des bulles et du texte : quels adjectifs (anglais ou français) te viennent en tête pour décrire ses émotions ?

PICK AN ACTIVITY

Imagine Seiji's answers to his coach in vignettes 2 and 3 above.

Act out the scene with six friends.

HELP

Écoute certains mots de la page et entraîne-toi à les prononcer avant de jouer !

Audio 22nefe5521

To be continued on p. 116

PROJECT

6

Take a Super Tour of New York City

Dans ce chapitre, tu vas :

- Découvrir New York avec des guides privilégiés : les élèves du Lycée Français de New York et... Spider-Man !
- Apprendre à parler de cette ville de tous les records.

Vocabulaire

- La ville
- Les lieux touristiques

Grammaire

- Le superlatif de supériorité
- Le comparatif de supériorité

JEU NUMÉRIQUE

Find the monument!

Follow your guides
around one of the most exciting cities
in the world!

LESSON 1

Discover NYC from above

1 Meet Spider-Man, a true New Yorker

B

"Behold, true believers!
The Amazing Spider-Man!
By night, he's a crime-fighting superhero on the streets of New York. But by day he's Peter Parker, a regular teen, just like you!"

The New Yorker, July 5, 2019

Peter Parker (*right*), in *Spider-Man Homecoming*, 2017

1 IN PAIRS **How much do you know about the man in the mask?**

a. Use the documents above to complete a spidergram about him. →

HELP

- Fais des liens entre les images et les textes.
- Regarde bien les décors.

b. Do you know more about this man? Add it to the spidergram.

2 **Share with the class.** Complete a giant spidergram!

Time to write

Add information to text B about the character's double identity. WB p. 63

2 Follow the guide!

1 Look at the two photos. Do you know the monument and the place they show?

2 Listen to a young American talking about them.

Audio 22nefe5601

a. Check your guesses and spot these places on the map. WB p. 64

b. Listen again. Choose one place and memorise as much information as you can.

c. Share with the class and fill in the cards in your workbook. WB p. 64

3 IN GROUPS **Discover more about NYC.** WB p. 65

4 What do you think about NYC? What is the most exciting place to visit for you?

MINI TASK!

Let's play!

Choose one of the places or monuments you have discovered and describe it to a classmate. Can he/she identify it and spot it on the map?

It's one of the most. . . .

Oh, it's. . . !

Dans cette leçon, tu as appris :

Vocabulaire ≫ p. 110
- La ville
- Les lieux touristiques

Grammaire ≫ p. 112
- Le superlatif de supériorité

LESSON 2

Meet New Yorkers

1 What is the best thing about NYC?

The five boroughs of New York City

Meet Josephine
Video 22nefe5604

Meet Kayo
Video 22nefe5603

1. **Look at the pictures above.** What can you guess about Josephine and Kayo?
2. **Watch the opening of each video.** Were you right? Start filling in a page from their scrapbooks. WB p. 66-67
3. IN GROUPS **a. Get ready to know more about Kayo.** WB p. 66
   b. Share what you have understood with the class.
4. **Watch Josephine's video and fill in her scrapbook page.** WB p. 67
5. IN GROUPS **Based on what you have heard, vote for:**

the best place | the best restaurant | the most exciting activity | the best time of the year

2 Play This or that?

Burgers or hot dogs?

Manhattan or Brooklyn?

Students play "This or That in NYC" Video 22nefe5605

1. **Look at the questions above.** What would *you* answer?

2. IN GROUPS **Watch the students play.**
   a. Tick the right box every time something gets a vote. WB p. 68-69

   b. Share with the class. For each pair, which element is the winner?

3. **Focus on <u>one pair</u>.** Try to understand the reasons for the students' preferences. WB p. 69

4. **React.** Based on their preferences, who are you most similar to? Lucia, Josephine, Kayo or Imran?

Time to write Use what you have learned to imagine Lucia's reasons for her preferences. WB p. 69

MINI TASK !

Play "This or that?" with your classmates. IN GROUPS

- Use the cards provided. WB p. 125
- Some of them are blank, so that you can create your own cards.

burgers...

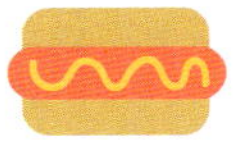
...or hot dogs?

New York in the winter...

... or in the summer?

Dans cette leçon, tu as appris :

Vocabulaire p. 110
- La ville

Grammaire p. 113
- Le comparatif de supériorité

FINAL TASK!

IN GROUPS

Imagine you're studying at Lycée Français de New York. Take part in an interview about life in NYC.

» Pense à utiliser le vocabulaire p. 110.

1 Recap what you know about New York City.

Think of what you have discovered thanks to:

the students from Lycée Français | Spider-Man

2 List your preferences.

Make up your mind about: the best places to visit | what is better: Manhattan or Brooklyn, etc. | the best restaurants | the best time of the year

3 Anticipate the questions. Imagine your answers.

best restaurants?

Momofuku's ramen bar in Soho

4 Pick the questions and answer them.

What is the best place to eat in New York?

The best restaurant for me is definitely Momofuku's ramen bar in Soho.

- Tu peux prendre part à cette interview en classe avec des camarades qui te poseront des questions,

OU

piocher les questions chez toi et te filmer, comme Kayo, Josephine et les autres.

- Tu peux garder ton identité ou bien choisir un prénom américain 🙂
- Tu peux porter des vêtements ou des accessoires typiquement new yorkais.

NEED HELP? Follow the guide!

NEED HELP?

Entraîne-toi à donner ton opinion et à justifier tes choix.

1 Comment exprimer son opinion? Audio 22nefe5606

a. Écoute les élèves du lycée français de New York et repère les expressions qui indiquent l'opinion.

b. Entraîne-toi à dire ces phrases à ton tour en faisant attention à la prononciation et à l'intonation.

Constitue ta propre petite liste d'expressions à employer pour donner ton avis.

In my opinion, the Met is better than the MoMA.

2 Comment justifier ses choix ? Audio 22nefe5607

a. Écoute les jeunes New Yorkais et identifie :

leur opinion → leur justification ; les mots pour introduire la justification

b. Entraîne-toi à dire ces phrases à ton tour en faisant attention à la prononciation et à l'intonation.

I prefer the subway because it's cheaper than a cab.

3 Et maintenant, à ton tour !

Entraîne-toi à donner ton opinion et à la justifier à partir des sujets suivants, ou d'autres de ton choix :

- The museum or the cinema?
- Maths or history?
- Spider-Man or Luke Skywalker?
- Skatepark or shopping mall?

Te voilà fin prêt(e) pour la FINAL TASK!

- Tu peux t'aider des pages 112-113 de ton manuel pour construire des comparatifs et des superlatifs.

WORDS

Apprends ces mots avec leur prononciation !

In the city

Audio 22nefe5608

a bridge

a park

a **ri**ver

a square
/eə/

an **a**venue,
a street

a block = *un pâté de maisons*

a **dis**trict, a **bo**rough,
a **neigh**borhood

Means of transport

a cab

the **sub**way

a **sto**ry
= a floor

a **buil**ding,
a **sky**scraper

Places of interest

Audio 22nefe5609

a **li**brary
/aɪ/

a **book**store

a mu**se**um
/juː/

paintings
art pieces
sculptures

sports fa**ci**lities

a show, a **mu**sical

theater, **o**pera,
bal**let**

a **res**taurant
/'restərɒnt/

location

Audio 22nefe5610

Up**per** West side

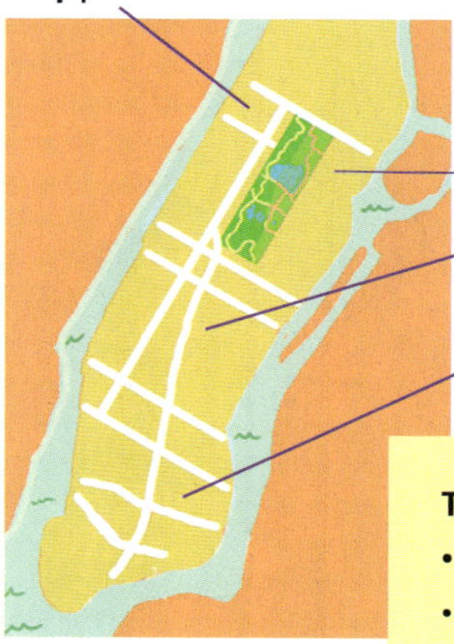

Upper East side

midtown,
downtown (US)

Lower East side

Touring

- **vi**sit
- go **sight**seeing
- a view

Describing places

Audio 22nefe5611

great, a**ma**zing,
im**pres**sive, **awe**some
/'ɒsəm/

ex**ci**ting,
pleasant

famous, **well**-known
/eɪ/

huge, high, tall
/hju:dʒ/

crowded, **bu**sy
/ɪ/
≠ calm, re**lax**ing

La ville

1 Top 10 des lieux touristiques !

a. Retrouve le mot manquant pour chaque pancarte.

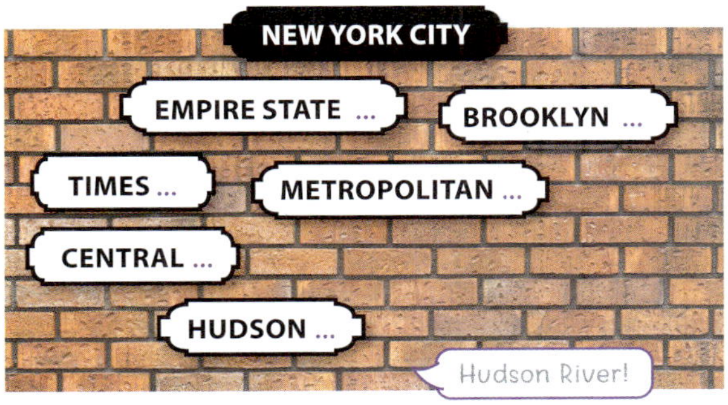

b. Défi ! Peux-tu faire la même chose avec ces lieux touristiques situés à Londres ?

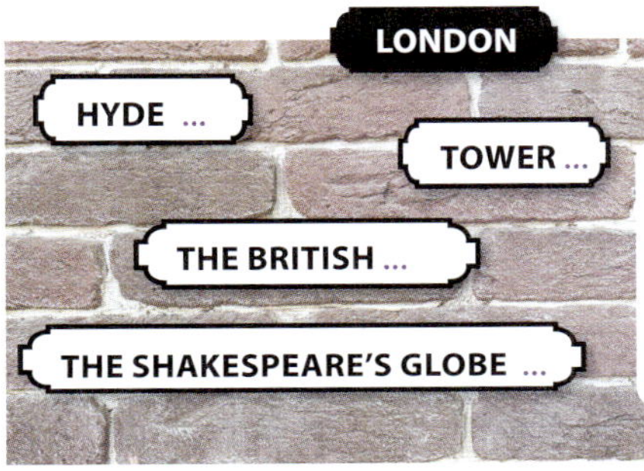

HELP
bridge
museum
park
theatre

2 Dictation time! Audio 22nefe5612

Écoute et écris les mots que tu entends.

3 New York est aussi la ville préférée des Avengers. Choisis un des personnages et imagine les raisons pour lesquelles il ou elle aime cette ville.

Inscris ce petit texte dans une jolie bulle de BD.

4 Listen up! Audio 22nefe5613

Écoute Lucia parler de ses activités favorites à New York. Crée un nuage de mots en notant tout ce qu'elle aime faire !

5 Ton professeur organise un voyage scolaire à New York. Il laisse à la classe le choix du lieu pour la première journée. Écris-lui un mail pour indiquer ta préférence.

Pense à justifier ton choix !

The Empire State Building

Times Square

Dear Mr Brown,
I prefer visiting ... because...

6 Prononciation Audio 22nefe5614

Les sons /ɑː/, /eɪ/, /æ/

a. Écoute les mots suivants et classe-les selon la prononciation du [a] :

park - avenue - cab - famous - large - art - skyscraper - amazing

/ɑː/ car	/eɪ/ state	/æ/ map
...	...	...

b. Entraîne-toi à les prononcer.

Poursuis l'entraînement
WB p. 70

Le superlatif de supériorité

➡ On l'utilise pour dire qu'un élément est supérieur au groupe dont il fait partie.

New York. The best, most exciting city on Earth.

➡ Sa construction dépend de la « taille » de l'adjectif.

The Statue of Liberty is not the tallest building in NYC, but it is the most iconic.

adjectif long : *the most* + adjectif

adjectif court : *the* + adjectif + *-est*

⚠ Certains adjectifs ont un superlatif de supériorité irrégulier :
good, well → *the best* *bad* → *the worst*
far → *the farthest/furthest*

Court ou long ?

- Les adjectifs d'**une syllabe** sont considérés comme **courts**.
- La plupart des adjectifs de **deux syllabes ou plus** sont considérés comme **longs**.
- Certains adjectifs de **deux syllabes**, notamment ceux terminés par ***-y***, ***-er*** et ***-ow***, fonctionnent comme des adjectifs courts.
  pretty → *the prettiest*
  clever → *the cleverest*

1 ★ Es-tu un super-héros de l'orthographe ? Écris le superlatif de supériorité de ces adjectifs :

Exemple : *big* → *the biggest*

busy | crowded | impressive | amazing | cool | large | good | famous | big

2 ★★ Contribue au *Guinness World Records* ! Utilise ces informations pour rédiger quatre courts articles sur des lieux incroyables à New York.

The Flatiron	unusual building	shaped like an iron[1]!
The Verrazzano Bridge	long bridge	2,200 meters long
Brooklyn	populated borough	2.5 million people
Central Park	large urban park	3.4 square kilometers
One World Trade Center	high building	1.776 feet[2]

1. an iron: *un fer à repasser* 2. 1 foot = 0,3 m

Exemple :

The Flatiron is the most unusual building in NYC. It is shaped like an iron!

3 ★★ Central Park est aussi connu pour les statues qui le peuplent. En voici quatre. Écoute la description de l'une d'elles et identifie-la. Audio 22nefe5615

Alice in Wonderland
Inspired by Lewis Caroll's characters

Romeo and Juliet
Inspired by William Shakespeare's characters

The Falconer

Hans Christian Andersen
The author of The Little Mermaid *and* The Ugly Duckling

LESSON 2

Le comparatif de supériorité

On l'utilise pour comparer deux éléments entre eux.

Manhattan is better than Brooklyn.

Sa construction dépend de la « taille » de l'adjectif.

The Met is **bigger** than the MoMA and the art pieces are **more** historical.

adjectif court : adjectif + *-er* + *than*

adjectif long : *more* + adjectif + *than*

- **On ne met pas *than* quand le deuxième élément de comparaison est sous-entendu.**

Certains adjectifs ont un comparatif de supériorité **irrégulier** :
good, well → better than   *bad → worse than*
far → further than

Attention à l'orthographe !

- Quand l'adjectif se termine par un **-e**, on ajoute seulement un ***-r*** :
  nice → nicer
- Quand l'adjectif comporte une syllabe et se termine par « consonne-voyelle-consonne », on double la dernière consonne :
  hot → hotter
- Quand l'adjectif se termine par un **-y**, on le transforme en ***-i-*** :
  happy → happier

1 Révise ta géographie !

a. Compare ces métropoles.

HELP
populated • large • high population density

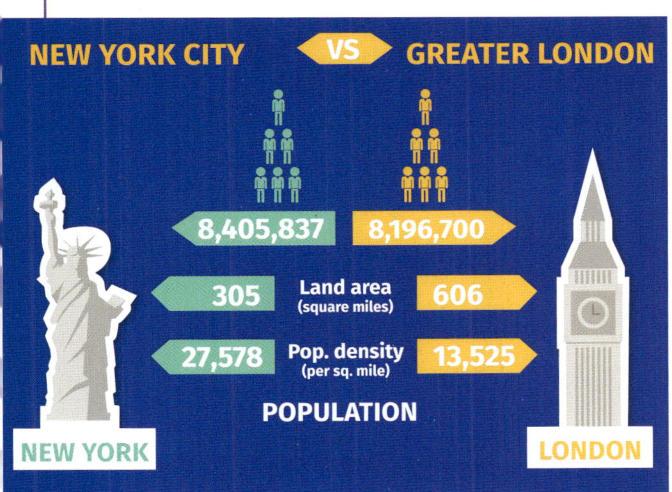

www.6sqft.com

b. Rédige deux questions que tu pourras poser à ton professeur lors du prochain cours de géographie.

HELP
expensive
green
young ...

Which city is... ? London or New York?

2 *This or that?*

À la manière des élèves du lycée français, réponds aux questions et justifie tes choix.

Bagel or burger?

The Statue of Liberty or Central Park?

Broadway show or Basketball game?

HELP
good
interesting
fun
exciting ...

3 Utilise tes connaissances du chapitre pour tester tes camarades ! Réalise une cocotte en papier avec des questions comparant deux lieux.

Exemple : *Which bridge is longer? Manhattan Bridge or Brooklyn Bridge?*

N'hésite pas à utiliser des informations découvertes dans les exercices.

Poursuis l'entraînement
WB p. 72

Choose your activities!

Early finishers

New York Quiz

How well do you know NYC?

1. **Which of these is a nickname for NYC?**
   a. The Giant Peach
   b. The Big Apple
   c. The Massive Raspberry

2. **Where does the Statue of Liberty come from?**
   a. England
   b. The US
   c. France

NYC Jokes

Why do cows go to New York City?

To see the MOO-sicals. (musicals)

Which building does Dracula visit in New York?

The Vampire State Building

Super facts about Spider-Man

Spider-Man, created by Stan Lee and Steve Ditko, first appeared in August 1962 in the Marvel comic book *Amazing Fantasy*.

Spider-Man was a great role model for young people. He was the first teenhero who wasn't just an adult's sidekick!*

* *acolyte*

Former President Obama's favorite superhero is actually Spider-Man.

Spider-Man's web disappears after an hour and yet is strong enough to carry the Hulk!

Spider-Man wasn't the only amazing hero in his family; his parents were spies and died in a plane crash. This is why Peter lived with May and Uncle Ben.

www.thefactsite.com

3 **How many skyscrapers are there in NYC?**
a. about 50
b. about 300
c. more than 1000

Paris only has 17 skyscrapers!

4 **What bridge connects Manhattan to Brooklyn?**
a. Brooklyn Bridge
b. Manhattan Bridge
c. Express Bridge

5 **How many subway lines are there?**
a. 18
b. 22
c. 36

6 **How many languages are spoken in NYC?**
a. about 20
b. about 100
c. more than 600

7 **When was NYC founded?**
a. in 1624
b. in 1664
c. in 1698

8 **What is Broadway mostly known for?**
a. famous store
b. theaters
c. museums

Answers: 1. b - 2. c - 3. b - 4. a - 5. c - 6. c - 7. a - 8. b

Bagel or burger?

Bagel!

The bagel arrived in the United States in the late 19th century with Jewish immigrants from Poland. It was sold on the streets of New York City's Lower East Side piled up on long sticks or hung from strings — that's why they have a hole — for people to buy and enjoy on the street. It was simple, comforting food.

Adapted from the freelibrary.com

Create your own bagel!

Choose from these ingredients:

bacon | egg and cheese | salad | burger | avocado and poached egg | egg salad | tuna | mozzarella | pesto and tomato | pastrami

Previously in *FENCE* ...

Nicholas has lost his match against Seiji, but he has not lost his passion for fencing...

HELP

- Pour comprendre ce nouvel épisode de la vie de Nicholas, regarde bien la première vignette.
- Quelle surprise attend Nicholas à son arrivée dans sa chambre ? Regarde cette vignette 🙂
- Pour comprendre ce que ressentent Nicholas et Seiji, regarde bien :
  – l'expression de leurs visages,
  – les symboles utilisés par le dessinateur dans les deux dernières vignettes,
  – ce que chacun dit.

PICK AN ACTIVITY

Discuss with a friend: why do Nicholas and Seiji not give the same answer in the last vignette?

Imagine you can go to a boarding school like this one to practise a sport. What sport would you choose? Who would be your roommate?

1. settle in : *s'installer* – 2. a scholarship student: *un boursier*
3. your scholarship [...] the team = *tu ne conserves ta bourse que si tu intègres l'équipe officielle de l'école*
4. try out for the team = *passer des tests de sélection pour intégrer l'équipe*

To be continued on p. 132

PROJECT

7

A land of festivals

Dans ce chapitre, tu vas :

- Découvrir l'histoire et la culture de l'Inde à travers ses fêtes traditionnelles
- Contribuer à un guide touristique destiné aux enfants

Vocabulaire

- Les rituels des différentes fêtes
- Les relations familiales et amicales

Grammaire

- Les quantifieurs
- *WILL*

JEU NUMÉRIQUE
Edit your holiday video!

Are you ready to discover
the wonders of India?

LESSON 1

So many festivals!

1 Discover the most popular celebrations

WHY SO MANY FESTIVALS?

India is a country where hundreds of festivals are celebrated throughout the year. Since it is a land of many different cultures, traditions, religions, ethnicities and practices, the festivals celebrated in the country are varied, colourful and vibrant. Be it Holi, Diwali, Dussehra, Eid, or Christmas, each of them is celebrated with the same enthusiasm.

1 Holi

2 Durga Puja

3 Independence Day

1. **Look at the pictures and read the title.**
   What do the photos show?
2. **Read the text above.**
   What words seem to correspond to the pictures?
3. **Can you answer the question in the title: *Why so many festivals?*** WB p. 75
4. **Listen to young Indians talking about festivals in India.** Audio 22nefe5701
   a. Match each recording with the corresponding picture.
   b. Use what you have understood about the festivals to add captions to the pictures. WB p. 76
5. **Which festival looks the most exciting to you? Why?**

Hindi is the official language of India, with English being the second official language.
Namaste = *hello* in Hindi

2 My favourite holiday

www.kids-world-travel-guide.com

HOME COUNTRIES CONTINENTS FUN FACTS GAMES & QUIZZES TRAVEL TIPS

KIDS-WORLD-TRAVEL-

Essay Writing Competition 2018 Category: 8 – 11 years

Diwali, my favourite festival

by Pranavkrishna Bharanidharan.

My favourite holiday is Diwali. It is also called "The Festival of Lights." It is celebrated in October or November by Hindus in India and the Indian Diaspora. It originated more than 2,500 years ago.

On the day of Diwali, I like to visit a temple, where I pray to Mother Lakshmi. We worship Goddess Lakshmi for peace, prosperity, and wealth. […]

We light our homes with diyas, an oil lamp made from clay. […] This is one of the reasons that Diwali is called as "The Festival of Lights." This signifies the victory of good over evil and the dispelling* of darkness. We also share sweets with our friends and family.

There are many delicious milk sweets, cashew sweets, and almond sweets my family prepares, but out of all of these delectable desserts, my favourite is Gulab Jamun. It is a milk sweet soaked in a sugar syrup.

The most enjoyable part of Diwali for me and my most favourite part of Diwali, is lighting sparklers with my family. The magnanimous light of the sparklers and saying "Happy Diwali" to my family helps me find the true spirit of Diwali, which is togetherness.

* the end

1 Look at the document and identify:

its author | the subject of the text

2 IN GROUPS **Read the essay.**

Find out information about:

- Group 1 *the origins of this festival*
- Group 2 *its purpose*
- Group 3 *the different rituals*

3 Read the last paragraph again.

a. What is Pranavkrishna's favourite part?

b. What about you? Which part seems the best to you?

MINI TASK

Take part in the essay writing competition IN PAIRS

Write a short essay about the Holi festival.

Explain :

- when it is celebrated
- how it is celebrated (*rituals/decorations/food/atmosphere*)

Dans cette leçon, tu as appris :

Vocabulaire » p. 126
- Les célébrations et rituels

Grammaire » p. 128
- Les quantifieurs

Révisions
- Le superlatif → p. 129

LESSON 2

Celebrating family bonds

1 Discover Raksha Bandhan

Akshay Kumar is one of the most popular actors in Bollywood!

AUG 11

Akshay Kumar
@akshaykumar

A story that touches your heart so deeply & so instantly, it's the quickest I've signed a film in my career. Dedicating this film, #RakshaBandhan to my sister Alka & to the most special bond in the world... that of a brother and sister. [...]

Akshay Kumar
@akshaykumar

Growing up my sister, Alka, was my first friend. It was the most effortless friendship. #RakshaBandhan is a dedication to her and a celebration of that special bond. ❤ Day one of the shoot today, need your love and best wishes.

1 IN PAIRS **Collect clues!**

Look at the movie poster and read the tweets.
Can you guess:

what the movie is about? | what the Raksha Bandhan festival is about?

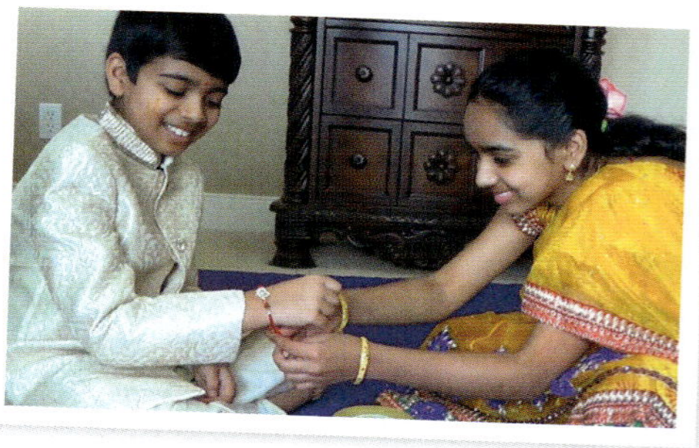

2 **Watch a video about the celebration of Raksha Bandhan.** Video 22nefe5702

a. Did you guess correctly?

b. Spot the different rituals.

3 **Make a word cloud about Raksha Bandhan.** WB p. 77

Time to write Write a short paragraph to explain what Raksha Bandhan is about and how it is celebrated. *Need help?* WB p. 77

2 Happy Raksha Bandhan!

1 Happy Raksha Bandhan my brother!!! This Raksha Bandhan, I promise to never stop teasing you, but whenever you need me in difficult times, I will always be there by your side to protect & support you.

2 My little sister, I don't know how life will take a turn but I promise you that the place you hold in my heart, no one ever will replace that. Happy Raksha Bandhan, sis!

3 We disagree. We fight. We argue. But my love for you is eternal. Happy Raksha Bandhan to you dear sister!

timesofindia.com, businessinsides.in

1 **Have a quick look at the documents above.** What do you think they are?

2 IN GROUPS

a. Choose a message and read it.

b. Check: who wrote it | to whom | what for

3 **Look for:**

a declaration of "love" or a promise WB p. 78

4 **Share your findings with the class.** What do you think of this ritual?

Time to write Discover more Raksha Bandhan messages, then write your own. WB p. 78

MINI TASK!

Celebrate Raksha Bandhan!

Just like an Indian teenager, write a message to your brother or sister or someone you love.

Dans cette leçon, tu as appris :

Vocabulaire p. 126
- Les relations familiales et amicales

Grammaire p. 129
- *WILL*

FINAL TASK !

IN GROUPS

Contribute to a travel guide for kids

Pense à utiliser le lexique p. 126

1 Choose your festival

Holi | Diwali | Durga Puja | Raksha Bandhan

2 Write your text

Tell the future travellers:

- Why Indian people celebrate this festival
- What they will see
- How they will celebrate the festival with Indian people

Why not write about Indian food? Write about what the travellers will taste during the festival!

3 Organize your web page

Design your page:

title of your text | name of the festival | pictures and illustrations | text

Make it attractive! 😊

NEED HELP? Follow the guide!

NEED HELP?

Organiser un travail d'écriture IN GROUPS

1 Relisez bien les consignes et planifiez votre travail.

Choix de la fête ?

Répartition du travail dans le groupe

Pourquoi ne pas s'appuyer sur les talents de chacun ?

Informations à donner ?

- origines et date de la fête
- rituels
- décorations/nourriture/ célébrations
- objectifs de la fête

2 Recherchez le vocabulaire dont vous aurez besoin.
Par exemple :

milk sweets
↓
prepare milk sweets

sparklers
↓
light sparklers

Utilisez les mots de la page WORDS p. 126, ou faites des recherches dans un dictionnaire bilingue.
→ wordreference.com par exemple

3 Rédigez les phrases puis enrichissez-les.
Par exemple :

— They prepare milk sweets.
— They prepare delicious milk sweets.
— They prepare a lot of delicious milk sweets.
— They prepare and share a lot of delicious milk sweets.
— They prepare and share a lot of delicious milk sweets with friends and family.

Enrichissez votre description et vos commentaires en ajoutant des détails.

4 Relisez-vous :
✔ Corrigez les fautes d'orthographe ou fautes de frappe
✔ Vérifiez la grammaire
Par exemple :

Le nom de la fête est bien orthographié.

J'ai utilisé la bonne préposition devant une date.

Je n'ai pas oublié la majuscule au mois.

Diwali is celebrated on November 4th.

WORDS

Apprends ces mots avec leur prononciation !

Rituals

Audio 22nefe5703

India specials

dance

sing re**li**gious songs
/rɪˈlɪdʒəs/

pray, pray to a god / **god**dess
visit a **tem**ple

throw **co**loured **pow**der
/θrəʊ/ /ˈpaʊdəz/

light **spark**lers,
light oil lamps
(diyas)

tie a **wrist**band
/aɪ/
promise to pro**tect**

Fun time together

Audio 22nefe5704

celebrate

decorate
the house with... **gar**lands

flowers

offer gifts

pre**pare** and share sweets
/prɪˈpeə/

write **mess**ages
/ɪz/

Relationships

Audio 22nefe5705

a **re**lative, a **fa**mily **mem**ber

a **si**bling = a **bro**ther or a **sis**ter
a bond (*un lien*)

pro**tect**
sup**port**
ad**vise**
/ədˈvaɪz/
stand by **so**meone
be there by **so**meone's side

fight, **ar**gue

a**gree** ≠ **dis**agree

tease,
make fun of **so**meone

Fêtes et rituels

1 Comment célèbre-t-on ces fêtes ?

Raksha Bandhan

Diwali

Pour chaque image :

a. ✱ **Nomme l'objet.**

b. ✱✱ **Fais une phrase.**

Holi

Exemple :

a. sparklers

b. For Diwali, people light sparklers.

2 ✱✱ **Comment célébrer Diwali ? Un intrus s'est glissé dans chacune de ces listes. Cherche-le puis remplace-le par une vraie tradition.**

1. visit a temple - prepare lots of pizzas - light diyas
2. offer gifts - write messages - go to the beach
3. sing - skate - pray
4. light sparklers - hang garlands - carve pumpkins

3 ✱✱✱ **Complète cet article d'un site de voyage.**

Holi, the festival of colors!

Held in March, Holi ... the arrival of spring. People gather in the streets and ... coloured powder. Children ... with water guns and balloons.

In the evening, people dress up and visit their ... . They ... sweets and drinks, and sometimes they ... on popular Holi songs.

4 **Listen up!** Audio 22nefe5706

✱✱✱ **Écoute Noe et trouve la fête dont il parle.**

a. **Note ce que tu comprends.**

b. **Écris un paragraphe pour expliquer cette fête à un ou une camarade.**

Relations familiales et amicales

5 **Dans un "Rakhi wish", on promet de chérir son frère ou sa sœur... en dépit des petites disputes.** 😉

a. ✱ **Dans quelle catégorie classerais-tu les verbes suivants ?**

support – agree – argue – protect– disagree – stand by

🙂	🙁
...	...

b. ✱✱ **Voici un exemple de "Rakhi wish". Classe les verbes qu'il contient dans le tableau ci-dessus.**

Cherche les mots que tu ne connais pas dans un dictionnaire !

rakhibazaar.com

We giggle and we cry, we play and we fight. The moments of happiness and sorrow we shared together have made our bond stronger. Wishing you a very Happy Raksha Bandhan.

6 **Listen up!** Audio 22nefe5707

✱✱✱ **Écoute Noe parler d'une autre fête. Laquelle est-ce ? Note ce que tu apprends sur ses frères et sœurs et sur la façon dont il célèbre cette fête avec eux.**

7 **Prononciation** Audio 22nefe5708

a. **Écoute ces adjectifs en faisant bien attention à leur prononciation. Que remarques-tu ?**

de**li**cious - re**li**gious

b. **Écoute à présent d'autres adjectifs terminés en *-ious* et répète-les.**

hi**la**rious - pres**ti**gious - **se**rious - super**sti**tious - **va**rious - am**bi**tious

Prononciation des adjectifs terminés en *-ious*

- L'accent est placé sur la syllabe **qui précède** le suffixe *-ious*.
- La terminaison *-ious* /əs/ ne s'entend presque pas. On dit qu'elle est réduite.

Poursuis l'entraînement
WB p. 79

Les quantifieurs

➡ **Pour parler de quantités, grandes ou petites, on utilise des quantifieurs.**

We prepare lots of sweets.

We spend a little time together

➡ **Certains quantifieurs s'utilisent uniquement avec :**

- **des noms dénombrables**

Brothers and sisters exchange a few gifts. There are too many fireworks.

noms dénombrables au pluriel

- **des noms indénombrables**

Have a little mango lassi! Holi is so much fun!

noms indénombrables (toujours au singulier)

Pour parler de...	On utilise...	
petites quantités	**a few** + nom dénombrable	**a little** + nom indénombrable
grandes quantités	**many** + nom dénombrable	**much** + nom indénombrable
	a lot of / lots of	

1 ★ **Complète ces phrases avec un quantifieur.**

a little | a few | many | a lot of

1. There are ... festivals and celebrations in India.
2. Holi, the festival of colours, is celebrated with ... fervor across the country.
3. I was lucky to arrive in India just ... days before Diwali.
4. "Mum, can you give me ... money so I can buy sparklers?"

2 ★★ **Remplace les éléments soulignés par l'un de ces quantifieurs.**

a lot of | many | a few

1. 50 festivals are celebrated each year in India.
2. My mother will only let me have 2 or 3 sweets... How frustrating!
3. There are more than 50 people at the party! What a success!
4. For Christmas, we only hang 2 or 3 fairy lights to decorate the house, but it's lovely.
5. My aunt is amazing: she can speak 6 or 7 languages.

3 ★★ **Un peu de géographie !**

Regarde ce graphique et ce poster :

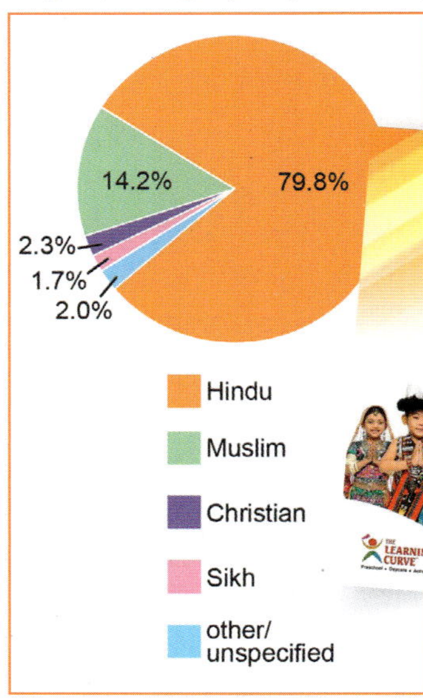

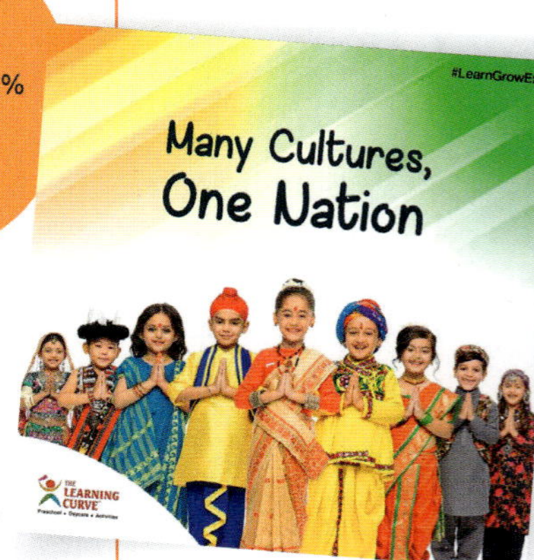

Commente ces documents en utilisant des quantifieurs. *Exemple :*

There are ... different religions in India, that's why there are so ... festivals.

LESSON 2

WILL

➡ On utilise *will* pour se projeter dans l'avenir et parler de ce qui a de fortes chances de se réaliser, par exemple, une promesse.

"What will you promise?" (promise: BV)

"I promise I will always be there by your side." (be: BV)

"I will not tease you anymore." (tease: BV)

Comme *CAN*, *WILL* est un auxiliaire modal :
- Il accompagne un verbe qui est toujours à la base verbale.
- Il sert à construire les questions et les négations.
- ***WILL* ne change pas**, quel que soit le sujet : → *I will help..., he will write ...*

➡ À l'oral, *will* est généralement contracté :

I'll always protect you. (↑ will)

I won't celebrate Raksha Bandhan without you! (↑ will not)

1 ✱ **a. Lis ces promesses d'un frère à sa sœur. Trouve celle qu'il dit « pour rire ».**

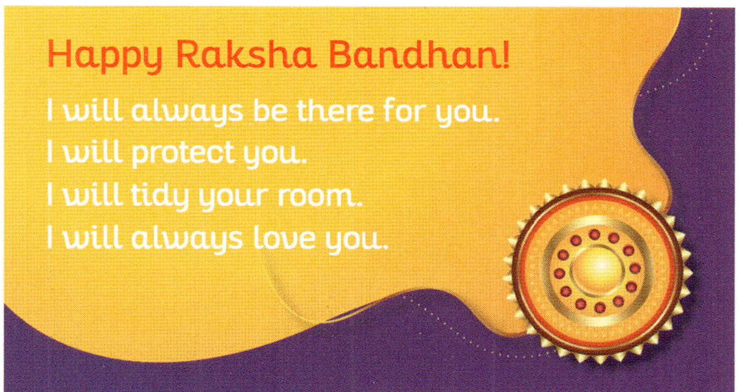

b. ✱✱ **À ton tour, écris tes promesses et glisses-en une pour rire.**

2 ✱✱ **Tu organises une grande fête pour le début des vacances d'été.**

a. Prépare ton invitation en indiquant ce que vous ferez.

dance | eat lots of candy | play with water guns | enjoy the pool

b. Mais il y a des choses que vous ne ferez certainement pas ! Ajoute deux exemples.

But we won't watch TV! 😉

3 ✱✱✱ **C'est le moment de prendre de bonnes résolutions ! Écris ce à quoi tu t'engages dans chacun des domaines ci-dessous.**

school | sport | food | family

Utilise tes connaissances ou cherche le vocabulaire qui te manque dans un dictionnaire.

School: I will do all my homework before I watch a movie.

4 ✱✱✱ **Ta grande sœur part étudier un an aux États-Unis. Pose-lui toutes tes questions !**

Will you phone me?

5 ***Le superlatif*** Révisions → p. 112

the most enjoyable - the quickest

✱✱ **Pour compléter ton article sur les fêtes indiennes, choisis un adjectif et mets-le au superlatif.**

symbolic | big | colourful | long

1. Holi is .... festival in India.
2. Diwali is ... festival in India.
3. Raksha Bandhan is ... festival in India.
4. Navatari is the ... Hindu festival. It lasts nine consecutive nights!

Poursuis l'entraînement
WB p. 81

Choose your activities!

Early finishers

Did you know about... languages in India?

India has 22 recognized languages.

However, the official languages are English and Hindi.
India also has the world's second-largest population of English speakers, since most Indians speak their own regional language as well as English for easier communication.

Can you guess which country has the largest population of English speakers?

a. The UK
b. The USA
c. China

Answers: b. The USA

Do it yourself!

Rangoli

Rangoli is a colourful pattern created on the floor using coloured sand, powdered coloured rice, coloured rice, dry flour or flower petals.

Create a rangoli design

Make your rangoli

- Choose a place where you want to make your Rangoli
- Draw the grid
- Create your own design
- Fill the design with lentils, grains, flowers etc...

Have a little taste of India !

1

2

3

4

→ How much do you know about Indian food? Match each picture with its name.
naan – lassi – laddu - butter chicken

Drawing competition

Read the descriptions of three popular Indian goddesses.

Hindu Goddess Saraswati

Saraswati is the goddess of creativity, knowledge, arts, music, literacy, and education. She is highly creative, artistic, intellectual, and nonchalant. Sometimes, however, she can begin too many projects. She has a strong imagination and brings beauty into everything she does.

Hindu Goddess Lakshmi

Lakshmi is the goddess of prosperity, purity, chastity and generosity. Her four hands represent these four spiritual virtues. She sits on a lotus flower, and is normally surrounded by elephants. She is covered in jewellery.

Hindu Goddess Durga

Durga is the powerful warrior goddess who protects those around her. She is ambitious, and sometimes a bit competitive and impatient. She is naturally a strong leader. She uses her power for good and is a protector of others.

→ Your turn!
- Research another god or goddess.
- Draw them.
- Then present them to your classmates.

Did you know about...
Holi celebrations in the UK?

There are lots of Holi celebrations in the UK, organised by the large British-Hindu community. Celebrating festivals can be a good way for people to feel close to their families and cultural heritage. The city of Leicester has a large Indian population and is famous for its Indian festival celebrations every year. Children love to use their spray cans and cover each other in colour. Holi parades are also held and in the evening people visit their friends and relatives to exchange greetings and sweets.

Not so fun fact

Heavy pollution during Diwali occurs due to the burning of firecrackers. This practice also releases toxins which certainly makes it hard for people to breathe.

READING CORNER

Previously in *FENCE*...

Nicholas and Seiji have discovered they are roommates at Kings Row Boys School.

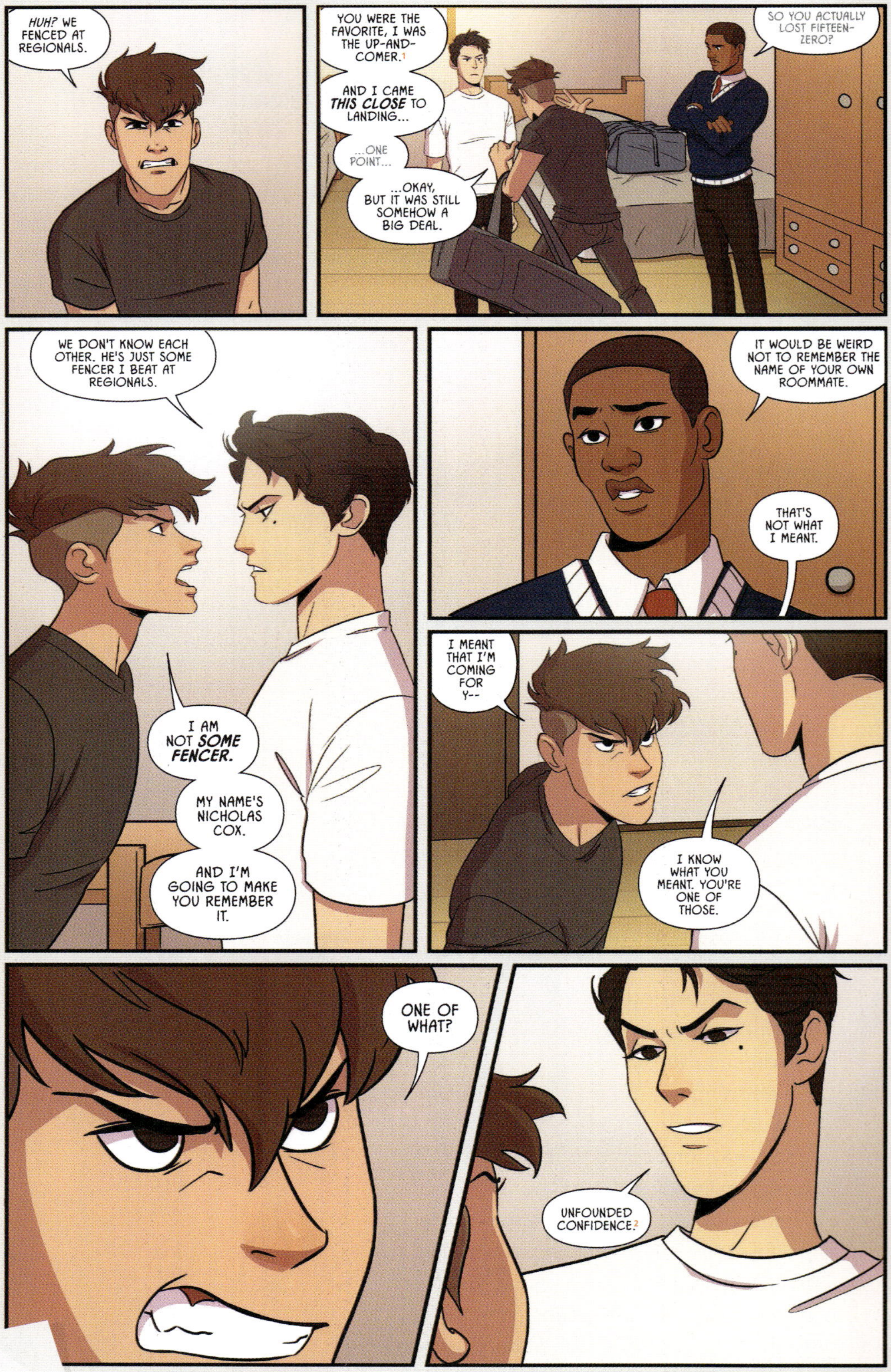

1. the up-and-comer = *l'étoile montante* – 2. *confiance injustifiée*

3. you haven't figured out yet = *tu n'as pas encore compris*
4. to room with someone = to share a room with someone
5. take it up with coach = discuss with coach

HELP

- La vignette 10 nous apprend une information capitale à propos de Seiji. Laquelle ?
- *Vignette 11* : Observe attentivement l'expression du visage de Seiji et repère le nom qu'il donne à Nicholas. Quelle semble être sa personnalité ?

PICK AN ACTIVITY

Imagine the meeting between Nicholas, Seiji and their coach in the morning, and act it out.

Act out the dialogue in vignettes 11 and 12.

To be continued on p. 148

PROJECT

8

Off to summer camp!

Dans ce chapitre, tu vas :

- Découvrir des *summer camps* incroyables aux États-Unis.
- Imaginer ton propre *summer camp* et convaincre tes camarades d'y participer !

Vocabulaire
- En colonie de vacances
- Activités de loisir

Grammaire
- *CAN*
- *Be going to*
- Révision : *WILL*

JEU NUMÉRIQUE
Summer Dobble

The holidays are coming!
What summer camp will you choose?

LESSON 1

Discover summer camps in the US

So much to do!

1 **Look at the pictures above.**
What do you learn about this place? location | participants | activities

2 **Watch the three videos.**
What do you think? Do you want to go there?

3 IN TEAMS **Choose a camp, then watch the corresponding video again.**

Waterfront Camp | Land Sports Camp | Summer Arts Camp

a. Tick the activities you can do there. WB p. 84

b. Now, challenge the other teams about your camp. How many activities can they remember?

Time to write Which is your favourite camp? Explain why.

MINI TASK

Choose your camp

1. Here are five logos of summer camps. Choose one.
2. Imagine what you can do there, then tell the class about your choice!

CIRCUS CAMP Greatest camp on earth!

ASTRO CAMP Summer Adventure Camp

CHOPPED CHALLENGE Summer Cooking Camp

SCHOOL of ROCK Summer Camp

PHOENIX FEATHER Magic Camp

I'd like to go to … camp because you can practise…

Dans cette leçon, tu as appris :

Vocabulaire p. 142
- Les activités de loisir
- En colonie de vacances

Grammaire p. 144
- CAN

LESSON 2

My time at camp

1 One camp, one memory!

Good-morning, Camp !

Ten-year-old Harry is spending a week at a summer camp in the Adirondack mountains with his brother Randy.

"Good morning, Camp Awonjahela!"

"Good morning, Mr. G," all the campers sang in unison.

"Fun, friendship, adventure, and safety!" Mr G. shouted.

"One camp, one memory!" the campers yelled back.

I raised my eyebrows in surprise at the weird little chant, but no one else seemed to mind.

"It's great to finally have everyone here with us," said Mr. G. […]

"Today is going to be a fantastic day at Camp Awonjahela. Swim tests will be this morning down at Lake Humphrey for the girls' cabins and any remaining boys who were late arriving. The annual tug of war* is after lunch, and throughout the rest of the day, we'll be rotating you through some of the group competition categories like archery, rifle range, crafts, outdoor cooking, karaoke, and boating.

Around us kids' faces lit up at the mention of the activities they liked the best. […]

"As the week progresses," said Mr G. "your counselors will keep a tally of your scores. The girls' and boys' cabin with the most points at the end of the week will be our camp champions."

Brother Wars, Cabin Eleven, by Steven K. Smith, 2018

* *tir à la corde*

1. **Look at the book cover and read the introduction.**
   What can you imagine about: the time of year | the place | the characters ?

2. **Read from line 1 to 8.**
   Draw the scene as you imagine it!
   Then share it with the class.
   Did you all understand the same thing?

3. *"Today is going to be a fantastic day at Camp Awonjahela."* (l. 8)
   Imagine why.

4. **Read the end of the text.**
   a. Pick out the activities mentioned.
   b. Would you like to go to this camp? Why or why not?

Time to write Complete today's schedule. WB p. 86

Today's schedule:

Time	Activity
8-9 am	Breakfast

2 "It's going to be awesome!"

Ruby talks about her summer camp
Video 22nefe5804

1 a. **Meet Ruby!** Listen to Part 1 (00 to 0:21).
Identify:

information about her | her opinion on summer camps

b. Share with the class and start completing Ruby's diary. WB p. 87

2 a. **Discover her plans for the summer!** Listen to Part 2 (0:22 to the end).
Collect information about: the camp | the activities

b. Share with the class and continue completing Ruby's diary. WB p. 87

Time to write Imagine Ruby's text message to her best friend as she tells her about her plans for the summer.

MINI TASK!

Deliver a welcome speech

1. **Choose another camp:**
   sports camp | music camp | theatre camp | ...
2. **Imagine the director's speech.**
   - Welcome the campers
   - Tell them about the activities at your camp
   - Tell them what they will get if they become camp champion

Good morning!
I'm Miss J. Welcome to you all.
This week is going to be fantastic!

Dans cette leçon, tu as appris :

Vocabulaire p. 142
- Les activités de loisir
- En colonie de vacances
- Les impressions, les sentiments

Grammaire p. 145
- *Be going to* + BV

Révisions
- WILL

FINAL TASK!

IN GROUPS

Create your own summer camp and convince your classmates to join in!

Pense à utiliser le lexique p. 142

1 Choose a type of camp

It can be related to outdoor or indoor activities:

arts | sports | science | literature | ...

2 Choose a name for your camp

It can be:

funny | serious | mysterious

3 Create a schedule

Be prepared to explain what campers are going to do on "a typical day at camp".

Think about all the activities you can do

Design a timetable

4 Present your camp as a counselor

Be welcoming.

Explain the programme.

Be enthusiastic!

5 Vote for your favourite summer camp.

NEED HELP?

Follow the guide!

NEED HELP?

Entraine-toi à faire une présentation

1 Rassemble et organise tes idées en anglais.

Pour présenter un summer camp

Our Summer Camp
- Place: near the sea
- Activities: water sports
- Schedule: . . .
- Accommodation: comfortable cabins
- Meals: . . .
- . . .

2 Comment vas-tu le dire en anglais ? Révise dans ton manuel.

Vocabulaire p. 142
- At the camp
- Indoor/outdoor activities
- Impressions

Grammaire p. 144-145
- *Can*
- *Be going to*
- *Will*

Connais-tu la prononciation des mots que tu vas employer ? Écoute les mots p. 142 ou cherches-en d'autres sur wordreference.com par exemple.

3 Fais ta présentation ! Annonce ce dont tu veux parler.

Do you want to discover a fantastic camp?

We're going to present the location, then the activities.

Écoute et répète. Audio 22nefe5805

4 Donne des détails. Ils permettront de visualiser ce dont tu parles.

At our camp there are 10 comfortable cabins.

Five counselors will be there for you.

Écoute et répète. Audio 22nefe5806

5 Essaie de captiver ton public !

- regarde tes camarades
- fais des pauses
- rends ton intervention vivante
- utilise des gestes pour mimer ce dont tu parles !

Te voilà fin prêt(e) pour la FINAL TASK !

WORDS

Apprends ces mots avec leur prononciation !

At the camp

Audio 22nefe5807

a **ca**bin

a **coun**selor

a **cam**per

have fun
/ʌ/
learn
dis**co**ver
practise
meet new **peo**ple
be your**self**
have new oppor**tu**nities

Impressions
- great = **awe**some
- u**ni**que
- unbe**lie**vable = in**cre**dible
- **cra**zy
- **frigh**tening = **sca**ry

Water sports (outdoor activities)

Audio 22nefe5808

ca**no**eing
/kəˈnuːɪŋ/

fishing

paddle **boar**ding

tubing
/juː/

snorkeling
/ɔː/

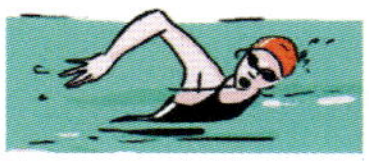

swimming

waterskiing

windsurfing

sailing

Land sports (outdoor activities)

Audio 22nefe5809

archery
/tʃ/ /i/

fencing

rock **clim**bing

hiking
/aɪ/

Arts (indoor activities)

Audio 22nefe5810

creative arts
/eɪ/
painting
pottery
jewellery **ma**king
/ˈdʒuːəlri/

culinary arts
/ˈkʌlɪnəri/
cooking
baking
cake **de**corating

performing arts
musical
/ju/
music / dance
drama
magic
circus

Parler du camp d'été

1 Cache la liste p. 142, et retrouve les noms correspondant à ces définitions :

1. a person who is in charge of young people at a summer camp
2. a small, simple house made of wood
3. a young person who goes to a camp during the summer

2 Dictation time! Audio 22nefe5811

Tu vas entendre 6 mots. Écris-les dans ton cahier en faisant bien attention à l'orthographe !

Parler des activités

3 IN PAIRS Mime une des activités apprises dans le chapitre. Ton ou ta camarade devra la nommer en anglais. Puis, échangez les rôles !

4 Chainspeaking
Répète les mots suivants et ajoute des activités de loisir.

Pourquoi ne pas jouer à 2 ?

C'est encore plus amusant !

fishing → canoeing → …

Fais la chaîne la plus longue possible !

5 Guess the sports! Audio 22nefe5812
Écoute 4 définitions. Pour chacune, trouve de quel sport il est question.

6 Tu es animateur de colonie. Recommande une activité à chacun de ces 5 participants.

1 I love to be in the water and to practise extreme sports. I think I'm a good swimmer.

2 I am very quick and I have excellent reflexes. I like the Three Musketeers.

3 I am not shy and I like being on stage. I can sing and dance.

4 I'm a very calm person who likes precision. Concentrating helps me relax. I never miss a target.

5 I really enjoy swimming but not diving in deep waters. I like fish, especially when they have lovely colours and shapes.

7 Que penses-tu des activités proposées dans ce camp ? Donne ton avis sur chacune d'elles en utilisant le vocabulaire proposé.

not very so really …	great awesome scary exciting fun amazing

Hiking is great! I love walking through nature.

8 Écris une carte postale à ton correspondant américain pour lui raconter ce que tu prévois de faire cet été.

Cite cinq activités

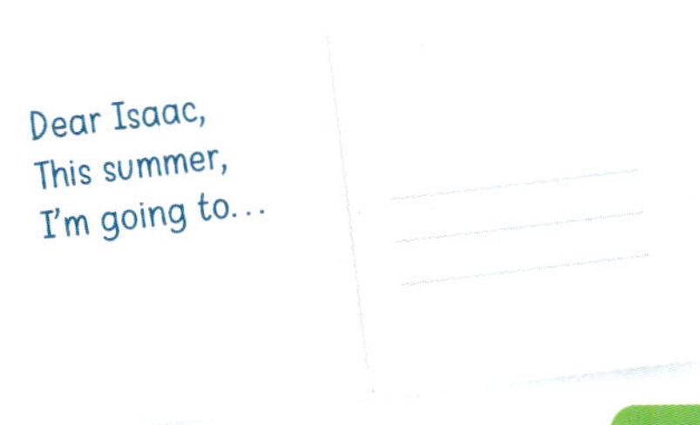

Poursuis l'entraînement WB p. 88

GRAMMAR

LESSON 1

CAN

➡ Pour parler de ce qui est possible ou permis, impossible ou interdit, on peut utiliser *CAN*.

You **can** make new friends.
You **can't** go canoeing alone.
base verbale
Can we bring food?

- *CAN* est un **auxiliaire modal** :
  - Il accompagne un verbe qui est toujours à la base verbale.
  - il sert à construire les questions et les négations.
- *CAN* **ne change pas**, quel que soit le sujet :
  → *I* ***can*** *sing..., he* ***can*** *dive..., they* ***can*** *swim...*

➡ *CAN* permet aussi de dire ce que l'on est capable de faire ou pas.

If you **can't** swim, you can try our summer arts camp.

can't = cannot
↑ forme contractée ↑ forme pleine

1 Dictation time!

Audio 22nefe5813

✱ **Écoute ces phrases puis complète-les.**

1. At camp you ... build memories that will last forever!
2. I ... sail but I ... waterski!
3. ... I phone my parents? Of course you ...!
4. She ... find her swimsuit, and the swimming lesson is in 5 minutes!
5. Why ... we stay up tonight? It's Saturday!

2 ✱✱ IN PAIRS Choisis l'un des quatre lieux ci-dessous. Ton / ta camarade doit te poser des questions pour deviner de quel lieu il s'agit.

Can you swim in this place?

No, you can't!

	cabin	bus	lake	campsite
play the guitar and sing	✓	✓	✗	✓
jump on the bed	✓	✗	✗	✗
swim	✗	✗	✓	✗
build a campfire	✗	✗	✗	✓

3 ✱✱ Explique aux participants de ce camp ce qu'ils sont autorisés à faire ou pas.

HELP
light a campfire

4 ✱✱✱ Tu es responsable d'un *summer camp* et tu recherches des animateurs. Prépare 5 questions à poser aux candidats pour savoir ce qu'ils savent faire ou pas.

5 Prononciation

Audio 22nefe5814

Écoute et répète ce dialogue.

I **can** come with you if you want me to!

Great, but can you surf?

Oh! No, I can't.

Ponunciation de ***can***

Affirmation	Question ou réponse courte	Négation
I **can** come /kən/	**Can** you surf? /kæn/ Yes, I **can**. /kæn/	I **can't** /kɑ:nt/

LESSON 2

BE GOING TO

➡ Pour parler de l'avenir, on peut utiliser *WILL*, comme tu l'as vu dans le chapitre 7, mais également *be going to*.

Today **is going to** be a fantastic day at Camp Awonjahela.
What **are** we **going to** do?
BE conjugué au présent — base verbale

➡ *be going to* s'utilise pour parler de ses intentions, ou pour faire une prédiction fondée sur une certitude ou sur une observation.

There are so many activities in this camp!
It**'s going to** be amazing!
It**'s not going to** be easy.

Prononciation
- À l'oral, *going* to se prononce parfois *gonna* /ˈgɒnə/. Tu entendras donc *"I'm gonna win!"*.
- Attention : cette prononciation relève de l'anglais familier, il ne faut pas l'écrire !

1 ✱ **Écoute et choisis les photos correspondant aux projets de Joe.** Audio 22nefe5815

1

2

3

4

2 ✱✱ **C'est ta première nuit en colonie. Imagine tout ce que tu vas faire demain... ou pas !**

stay in bed - wake up early - make new friends - stay alone – go rock climbing - go surfing - ...

I am not going to stay in bed late. I'm ....

3 ✱✱✱ **Question time**

a. Lis les questions suivantes et réponds-y.
1. What are you going to do next summer?
2. What are you *not* going to do?
3. Where are you going to spend the weekend?
4. What are you going to do after school tomorrow?

b. Rédige deux nouvelles questions pour tes camarades.

4 ✱✱✱ **Let's party! Ton ami(e) organise une fête. Pose-lui des questions pour en savoir plus !**
1. When ...
2. Who ...
3. What ...
4. How ...

HELP

have a party	food
invite (friends)	drinks
decorate (the house)	music

5 Prononciation Audio 22nefe5816

Écoute trois phrases. Quelle différence repères-tu ? Entraîne-toi à répéter ces phrases.

Les registres de langue à l'oral
- *gonna* est la contraction de *going to*.
- Quelle est la contraction de *want to* d'après toi ?

6 WILL Révisions → p. 129

Swim tests **will** be this morning.

✱✱ **Voici trois situations imaginaires. Imagine ce que tu décideras dans chaque cas.**

If school is cancelled today, I....

If I win $1000 on the lottery, I....

If I can have anything I want for dinner, I...

Poursuis l'entraînement WB p. 90

Choose your activities!

Early finishers

Special camps!

Read these summer camp names:

→ **Draw a logo for each of them.**
→ **Your turn. Combine two things that don't seem to go together to create new summer camps.**
Make them fun!

Weird but true

"Bug juice" is a super-sweet juice drink made with artificially flavored powder. It is very often served at summer camps in the US. Camp counselors tell the kids it is made from mashed-up bugs*!

* mashed-up bugs: *insectes écrasés*

Do it yourself!

Make s'mores!

Top* crackers with toasted marshmallows. Add caramel topping and chocolate; top with other crackers.

* top: *recouvrir*

A s'more is a very popular campfire snack in the United States and Canada!

→ **What is *your* favourite summer recipe?**
Write it (in English of course!) and illustrate it. Then swap with one of your classmates.

Summer poem

Secret message

Read these funny letters from young campers.

Can you find the hidden message in letter 1?

SECRET MESSAGE

I love and miss you.
I hate the woods.
Camp is cool.
Try to find the secret message.

We have to do everything, cook food, clean up, no lollies and we are locked up like prisoners.

→ **Your turn.** **Write a funny letter from a happy – or not-so-happy – camper!**

I can't wait for summer

I can't wait for summer, when school days are done,
to spend the days playing outside in the sun.
I won't have to study. No homework, no tests.
Just afternoons spent on adventures and quests.
Instead of mathematics and writing reports,
I'll go to the park and play summertime sports.
Instead of assignments, report cards, and grades,
I'll get to play baseball and watch the parades.
I'll swing on the playground. I'll swim in the pool
instead of just practicing lessons in school.
The second the school year is finally done
I'll spend every minute with friends having fun.
I hardly can wait for the end of the year.
I'm counting the days until summer is here.
It's hard to be patient. It's hard to be cool.
It's hard to believe it's the first day of school.

Kenn Nesbitt, 2005

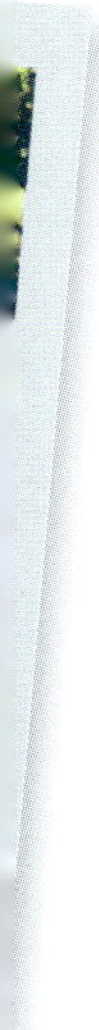

Camp riddle!

→ **Two fathers and two sons go fishing. They each catch a fish and return with three fish only. Why?**

There was a grandfather, a father and a son.

→ **Listen to this poem, then copy it in your notebook.** Audio 22nefe5817
Illustrate as many words as you can.

READING CORNER

Previously in *FENCE* ...

Seiji knows he is much better at fencing than Nicholas, but Nicholas is determined to improve. It's training time!

1. bout : fight, combat
2. wrist : *poignet*
3. forearm : *avant-bras*
4. stance : *posture*
5. to step : *faire un pas*
6. catch up : *rattraper ton retard*

HELP

- Pour connaître les points forts de Nicholas, lis attentivement la vignette 6 p. 148.
- Pour connaître ses points faibles, lis les vignettes qui suivent. Chacune est divisée en 2 : comprends-tu ce que montre chaque partie ?
- Comprends-tu pourquoi Nicholas se met en colère dans l'avant-dernière vignette ?

ACTIVITY

Read the last vignette: what will Nicholas answer? Imagine what happens next, write the story and illustrate it!

Nicholas va-t-il progresser ? Réussira-t-il à battre Seiji ? Si tu as envie de le savoir, n'hésite pas à lire le livre !

Annexes

Un projet de classe pour découvrir la Saint Patrick
et la célébrer au collège !

Un « kit » pour avoir sous la main les essentiels
de la grammaire en 5e !

Celebrate Saint Patrick's Day!

MARCH
17

Dans ce chapitre, tu vas :

- Découvrir les origines d'une fête irlandaise et la manière dont elle est célébrée,
- Organiser des activités pour la célébrer en classe.

Investigate Saint Patrick's Day!

Discover the celebration and its origins then complete the investigation report in your workbook! WB p. 93

1 Who was Saint Patrick?

Saint Patrick was born in England in the 4th century, but when he was a teenager, he was captured by Irish pirates who took him to Ireland as a slave. After six years, Saint Patrick escaped and returned to England and his family. When Saint Patrick became a priest, he traveled back to Ireland to teach the people about Christianity.
Saint Patrick's Day is a celebration of his memory. It originally started as a celebration of Christianity in Ireland, but today, it is a day of celebration of all things Irish.

Adapted from history.com

Did you know?

Saint Patrick didn't wear green. His colour was "Saint Patrick's blue." The colour green became associated with St. Patrick's Day after it was linked to the Irish independence movement in the late 18th century.

2 How is St Patrick's Day celebrated in Ireland?

Galway

Listen to some Irish music.

Video 22nefe5b01

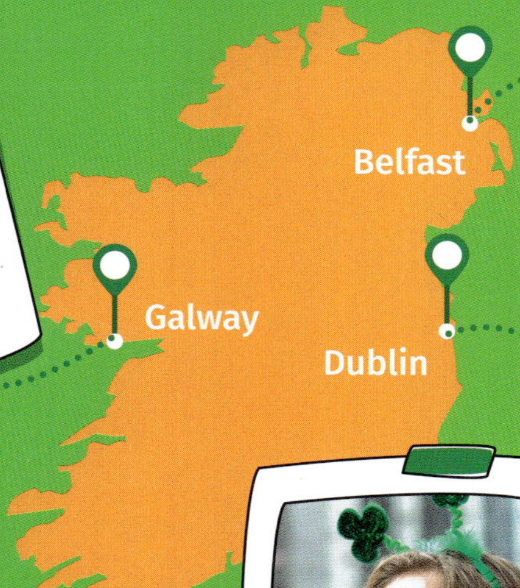

Belfast

Watch some traditional Irish dancing.

Video 22nefe5b03

Listen to a young Irish girl explain how she celebrates St Patrick's Day.

Audio 22nefe5b02

Dublin

3 ...and around the world?

In the 19th century, millions of Irish people left Ireland to find a better life abroad, mostly in the USA. But integrating was not always easy, as Irish immigrants sometimes faced discrimination. So the Irish community abroad felt the need to celebrate their heritage and culture. St Patrick's Day was a big part of it. Today, it is celebrated all around the world by millions of people!

17 March · Follow

Niall Burgess @NBurgessDFAT

No country has a day, a colour & a global community like Ireland, & none celebrates its culture more proudly. 500 landmarks now going green & 100 virtual celebrations hosted by @dfatirl missions #working4IRL worldwide. #GlobalGreening #GlobalIreland

Irish Foreign Ministry and Global Irish

Video 22nefe5b04

Watch the festivities in Chicago, voted best city to celebrate Saint Patrick's Day!

Audio 22nefe5b05

emigrate = leave your home country for another

an **im**migrant

integrate: *s'intégrer*

world**wide** *(adv.)* = all ar**ou**nd the world

a**broad** *(adv.)* = in / to an**o**ther **coun**try

Did you know?

In the USA, Irish immigrants began observing St. Patrick's Day in Boston in 1737 and the first St. Patrick's Day parade in America was held in New York City in 1766.

Let's Celebrate

Saint Patrick's Day!

Prepare the celebration

- Create some decorations
- Make a St Patrick's Day photobooth kit
- Decorate cookies
- Make a poster to advertise for the celebration

Before — **On D-Day** — **After**

Audio 22nefe5b06

dress up

put on **make**-up

a **le**prechaun

a **sham**rock

dance

play **mu**sic, **lis**ten to **mu**sic

dye = *teindre*

Celebrate in true Irish style!

- Take part in a parade
- Vote for the best costume
- Do some Irish dancing
- Listen to Irish music
- Play games

Write about the celebration

- Write a tweet about the celebration in your school (with pictures!)
- Why not publish it for real with the hashtags #Global-Greening or #StPatricksDay ?

Grammar Essentials

1 Les pronoms

Pronom personnel sujet		Pronom personnel complément	
I	*I like chocolate.*	me	*Have some with me!*
you	*You are late.*	you	*I'm waiting for you!*
she	*She is funny.*	her	*I like her.*
he	*He is my neighbour.*	him	*I live next to him.*
it	*It is very good.*	it	*I love it!*
we	*We need help.*	us	*Can you help us?*
you	*Lily and Bill, you are so nice!*	you	*Thank you!*
they	*They can surf.*	them	*Look at them!*

2 Les adjectifs possessifs

my	*My brother is funny.*
your	*I like your jacket.*
her	*Her bag is pink.*
his	*His bag is grey.*
its	*Its colour is red.*
our	*Our garden is small.*
your	*Kids, open your books, please!*
their	*I love their house.*

3 *BE* et *HAVE* au Présent

I am	I have
you are	you have
she/he/it is	she/he/it has
we are	we have
you are	you have
they are	they have

4 *BE* et *HAVE* au Prétérit

I was	I had
you were	you had
she/he/it was	she/he/it had
we were	we had
you were	you had
they were	they had

5 There + BE

Il y a / Il n'y a pas	Il y avait / Il n'y avait pas
There is + singulier • *There is a new girl in our school.* • *There isn't a new girl in our school.*	**There was + singulier** • *There was a car accident.* • *There wasn't a car accident.*
There are + pluriel • *There are 15 boys in the class.* • *There aren't 15 boys in the class.*	**There were + pluriel** • *There were many people on the bus.* • *There weren't many people on the bus.*

There + BE :
BE s'accorde avec le 1er nom qui suit.

6 Les mots interrogatifs

Utilise...	Pour demander...
Who	*Who are you?* (Qui es-tu ?) *Who's absent today?* (Qui est absent ?)
What	*What is the date?* (Quel jour sommes-nous ?) *What is it?* (Qu'est-ce que c'est ?) *What's wrong?* (Qu'est-ce qui ne va pas ?) *What's going on?* (Que se passe-t-il ?) *What are you doing?* (Que fais-tu ?)
What time	*What time is it?* (Quelle heure est-il ?)
When	*When did you see her?* (Quand l'as-tu vue ?)
Where	*Where is my bag?* (Où est mon sac ?)
Where... from	*Where are you from?* (D'où viens-tu ?)
Why	*Why is he angry?* (Pourquoi est-il en colère ?)
How	*How are you?* (Comment vas-tu ?)
How old	*How old are you?* (Quel âge as-tu ?)
How much	*How much is it?* (Combien ça coûte ?)
How many	*How many pupils are there in the class?* (Combien d'élèves y-a-t-il dans la classe ?)
Whose	*Whose book is it?* (À qui est ce livre ?)
How often	*How often do you practise?* (À quelle fréquence t'entraînes-tu ?)

7 Les adverbes de fréquence

Isaac **always** wakes up early.

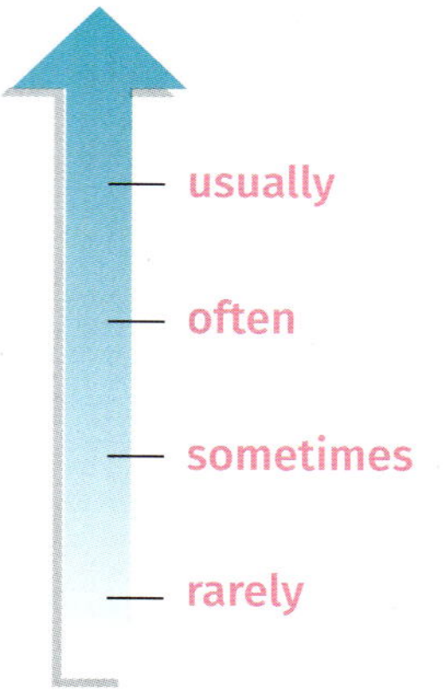

Isaac **never** wakes up early.

8 L'ordre des mots dans une question

Mot en *WH-*	Auxiliaire	Sujet	verbe	Suite...
Where	do	you	live?	
What	are	you	doing	tonight?
	Do	you	speak	English?
	Can	you	help	me?

9 Quelques auxiliaires modaux

Possible, permis / impossible, interdit	• *You can eat outside.* • *You can open the window.*	• *You can't eat outside.* • *You can't open the window.*
Obligations / interdictions	• *You must do your homework.* • *You must arrive on time.*	• *You mustn't forget your homework.* • *You mustn't arrive late.*
Expression du futur	• *I will visit NYC next summer!* • *I'll go to the cinema on Saturday.*	• *I won't visit L.A.* • *I won't go to the restaurant tonight.*

10 Les prépositions de lieu

a**bove**

at (*the bus stop*)

be**hind**

in **front** of

in the **mid**dle of

next to
= **close** to

be**tween**

far ≠ near

in = **in**side

on = on **top** of

opposite

up ≠ down

11 What time is it?

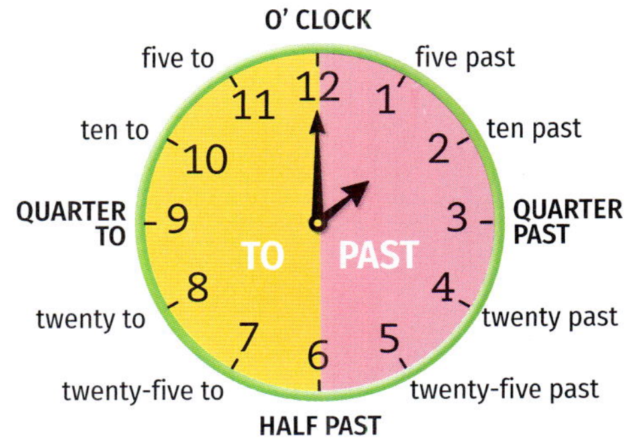

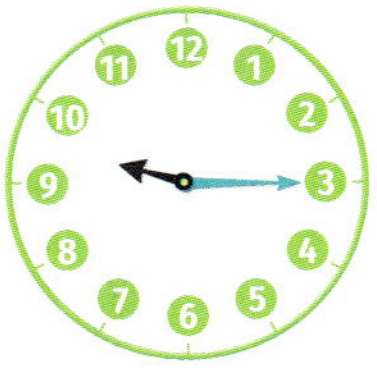
*It's **a** quarter past **nine**.*

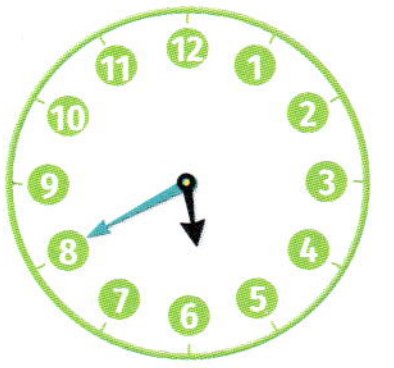
*It's twenty to **six**.*

Tu peux aussi dire : *It's nine fifteen* / *It's five forty*

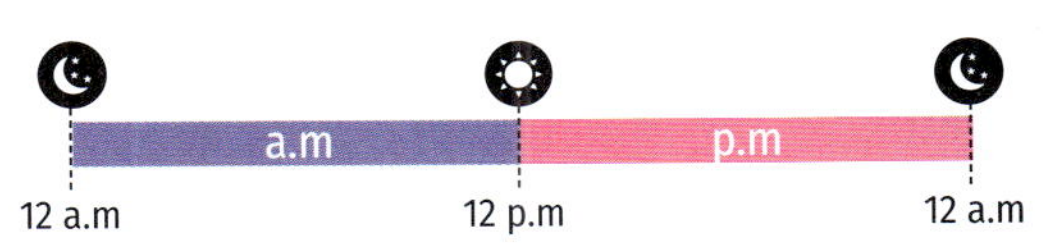

12 Le comparatif

	Construction	
Comparatif de supériorité	**adjectif court** + -(e)r + *than* OU more + **adjectif long** + *than*	• *This building is **big**ger than others.* • *I find the book more **interesting** than the film.*
Comparatif d'infériorité	less + **adjectif** + *than*	• *This tower is less **high** than the Empire State building*
Comparatif d'égalité	as + **adjectif** + as	• *My book is as **interesting** as yours.*

13 Les verbes irréguliers

Voici les verbes irréguliers les plus utilisés. Apprends-les avec leur prononciation.

Infinitif	Prétérit	Participe passé	Traduction
be /biː/	**was/were** /wɒz/ /wɜː/	**been** /biːn/	être
beat /biːt/	**beat** /biːt/	**beaten** /biːtn/	battre
become /bɪˈkʌm/	**became** /bɪˈkeɪm/	**become** /bɪˈkʌm/	devenir
begin /bɪˈgɪn/	**began** /bɪˈgæn/	**begun** /bɪˈgʌn/	commencer
bite /baɪt/	**bit** /bɪt/	**bitten** /bɪtn/	mordre
blow /bləʊ/	**blew** /bluː/	**blown** /bləʊn/	souffler
break /breɪk/	**broke** /brəʊk/	**broken** /ˈbrəʊkn/	casser
bring /brɪŋ/	**brought** /brɔːt/	**brought** /brɔːt/	apporter
build /bɪld/	**built** /bɪlt/	**built** /bɪlt/	construire
buy /baɪ/	**bought** /bɔːt/	**bought** /bɔːt/	acheter
catch /kætʃ/	**caught** /kɔːt/	**caught** /kɔːt/	attraper
choose /tʃuːz/	**chose** /tʃəʊz/	**chosen** /ˈtʃəʊzn/	choisir
come /kʌm/	**came** /keɪm/	**come** /kʌm/	venir
cost /kɒst/	**cost** /kɒst/	**cost** /kɒst/	coûter
cut /kʌt/	**cut** /kʌt/	**cut** /kʌt/	couper
do /duː/	**did** /dɪd/	**done** /dʌn/	faire
dream /driːm/	**dreamt** /dremt/	**dreamt** /dremt/	rêver
drink /drɪŋk/	**drank** /dræŋk/	**drunk** /drʌŋk/	boire
drive /draɪv/	**drove** /drəʊv/	**driven** /drɪvn/	conduire
eat /iːt/	**ate** /eɪt/	**eaten** /iːtn/	manger
fall /fɔːl/	**fell** /fel/	**fallen** /ˈfɔːlən/	tomber
feel /fiːl/	**felt** /felt/	**felt** /felt/	se sentir, toucher
fight /faɪt/	**fought** /fɔːt/	**fought** /fɔːt/	se battre
find /faɪnd/	**found** /faʊnd/	**found** /faʊnd/	trouver
fly /flaɪ/	**flew** /fluː/	**flown** /fləʊn/	voler (oiseau, avion...)
forget /fəˈget/	**forgot** /fəˈgɒt/	**forgotten** /fəˈgɒtən/	oublier
get /get/	**got** /gɒt/	**got** /gɒt/	obtenir
give /gɪv/	**gave** /geɪv/	**given** /ˈgɪvən/	donner
go /gəʊ/	**went** /went/	**gone** /gɒn/	aller
have /hæv/	**had** /hæd/	**had** /hæd/	avoir

Grammar Essentials

Infinitif	Prétérit	Participe passé	Traduction
hear /hɪə/	**heard** /hɜːd/	**heard** /hɜːd/	entendre
hide /haɪd/	**hid** /hɪd/	**hidden** /'hɪdən/	cacher
hit /hɪt/	**hit** /hɪt/	**hit** /hɪt/	frapper
hurt /hɜːt/	**hurt** /hɜːt/	**hurt** /hɜːt/	blesser
keep /kiːp/	**kept** /kept/	**kept** /kept/	garder
know /nəʊ/	**knew** /njuː/	**known** /nəʊn/	connaître, savoir
leave /liːv/	**left** /left/	**left** /left/	quitter, partir
make /meɪk/	**made** /meɪd/	**made** /meɪd/	faire, fabriquer
meet /miːt/	**met** /met/	**met** /met/	rencontrer
pay /peɪ/	**paid** /peɪd/	**paid** /peɪd/	payer
put /pʊt/	**put** /pʊt/	**put** /pʊt/	mettre
read /riːd/	**read** /red/	**read** /red/	lire
run /rʌn/	**ran** /ræn/	**run** /rʌn/	courir
say /seɪ/	**said** /sed/	**said** /sed/	dire
see /siː/	**saw** /sɔː/	**seen** /siːn/	voir
send /send/	**sent** /sent/	**sent** /sent/	envoyer
shut /ʃʌt/	**shut** /ʃʌt/	**shut** /ʃʌt/	fermer
sing /sɪŋ/	**sang** /sæŋ/	**sung** /sʌŋ/	chanter
sit /sɪt/	**sat** /sæt/	**sat** /sæt/	être assis
sleep /sliːp/	**slept** /slept/	**slept** /slept/	dormir
smell /smel/	**smelt** /smelt/	**smelt** /smelt/	sentir
speak /spiːk/	**spoke** /spəʊk/	**spoken** /'spəʊkən/	parler
spend /spɜnd/	**spent** /spɜnt/	**spent** /spɜnt/	passer, dépenser
take /teɪk/	**took** /tʊk/	**taken** /teɪkən/	prendre
tell /tel/	**told** /təʊld/	**told** /təʊld/	dire, raconter
think /θɪŋk/	**thought** /θɔːt/	**thought** /θɔːt/	penser
understand /ʌndə'stænd/	**understood** /ʌndə'stʊd/	**understood** /ʌndə'stʊd/	comprendre
wake /weɪk/	**woke** /wəʊk/	**woken** /'wəʊkən/	réveiller
win /wɪn/	**won** /wʌn/	**won** /wʌn/	gagner
write /raɪt/	**wrote** /rəʊt/	**written** /'rɪtən/	écrire

TABLE DES ILLUSTRATIONS / RÉFÉRENCES ICONOGRAPHIQUES

p. 4-hg1 ph © Cultura RM / Alamy Banque D'Images ; **p. 4**-hg2 ph © geogphotos / Alamy Stock Photo ; **p. 6**-hg ph © Adobe/eldadcarin ; **p. 7**-hg ph © Birch Path Literary, D.R ; **p. 8**-ph hd © © Adobe /Ilona Baha ; **p. 9**-hg ph © Adobe/Ruslan Gilmanshin ; **p. 9**-hd ph © Adobe/nerthuz ; **p. 10**-m ph © Striking Images - Tourism Ireland / Alamy Stock Photo ; **p. 12 & 13** ph © Getty Images / iStock / Ljupco; **p. 14**-1 ph © Entertainment Pictures / Alamy Banque D'Images ; **p. 14**-2 ph WENN Rights Ltd / Alamy Stock Photo ; **p. 14**-3 ph © Entertainment Pictures / Alamy Stock Photo ; **p. 14**-4 ph Collection Christophel © Village Roadshow Pictures / Warner Bros ; **p. 14**-5 ph © BBC / Collection Christophel ; **p. 14**-6 ph © Everett Collection / Aurimages ; **p. 14**-7 ph © Mary Evans / Aurimages ; **p. 14**-8 ph COLLECTION CHRISTOPHEL © Jersey Films ; **p. 14**-9 ph © Columbia Pictures/courtesy Everett Collection ; **p. 14**-10 ph ©United Archives GmbH / Alamy Stock Photo ; **p. 14**-11 ph © Joseph Prezioso / ZUMA Wire ; **p. 14**-12 ph COLLECTION CHRISTOPHEL © Warner Bros. / Heyday Films ; **p. 14**-13 ph Allstar Picture Library Ltd. / Alamy Stock Photo ; **p. 14**-14 ph © Danjaq / EON Productions / EVERETT / Aurimages ; **p. 14**-15 ph © WFPA / Alamy Stock Photo ; **p. 14**-16 ph COLLECTION CHRISTOPHEL © Walt Disney Pictures ; **p. 16**-hd1 ph © geogphotos / Alamy Stock Photo ; **p. 16**-hd2 ph © Cultura RM / Alamy Banque D'Images ; **p. 17**-1 ph MR. MENTM LITTLE MISSTM © 2012 THOIP (a SANRIO Company). All Rights reserved; **p. 17**-2 ph MR. MENTM LITTLE MISSTM ©2012 THOIP (a SANRIO Company). All Rights reserved ; **p. 17**-3 ph MR. MENTM LITTLE MISSTM ©2012 THOIP (a SANRIO Company). All Rights reserved ; **p. 17**-4 ph MR. MENTM LITTLE MISSTM ©2012 THOIP (a SANRIO Company). All Rights reserved ; **p. 19**- mg ph Collection Christophel © Village Roadshow Pictures / Warner Bros ; **p. 19**-md ph © Mary Evans / Aurimages ; **p. 21**-hg ph MR. MENTM LITTLE MISSTM ©2012 THOIP (a SANRIO Company). All Rights reserved ; **p. 22**-m1 ph © Danjaq / EON Productions / EVERETT / Aurimages ; **p. 22**-m2 ph COLLECTION CHRISTOPHEL © Warner Bros. / Heyday Films ; **p.22**_bd ph COLLECTION CHRISTOPHEL © British Broadcasting Corporation (BBC) - Home Box Office (HBO) - Bad Wolf - New Line Cinema - Scholastic ; **p. 23**-hg ph COLLECTION CHRISTOPHEL © Walt Disney Pictures ; **p. 23**-bg ph © illustration by Quentin Blake / United Agents 2016 ; **p. 23**-bd ph © clipartkey ; **p. 24**-md ph COLLECTION CHRISTOPHEL © Jersey Films ; **p. 26**-m WENN Rights Ltd / Alamy Stock Photo ; **p. 26**-b ph Leisan Gabidullina, ©BrightSide.me, D. R ; **p. 27**-h1 ph © WFPA / Alamy Stock Photo ; **p. 27**-h2 ph © Everett Collection / Aurimages ; **p. 27**-h3 ph COLLECTION CHRISTOPHEL © Walt Disney Pictures ; **p. 27**-h4 ph © WENN Rights Ltd / Alamy Stock Photo ; **p. 27**-m ph © Entertainment Pictures / Alamy Banque D'Images ; **p. 27**-b2 © Netflix / The Hollywood Archive ; **p. 27**-b3 ph Collection Christophel © 1492 Pictures / Heyday Films / Warner Bros ; **p. 28-29** ph © Icon Sportswire / Getty Images ; **p. 30**-hg ph © Adobe/Ilona Baha ; **p. 30**-m ph © Icon Sportswire / Rich von Biberstein / Icon Sportswire via Getty Images ; **p. 30**-b ph © H. Michael Miley / CC BY-SA 2.0 ; **p. 30-31**-m ph © Adam Lacy / Cal Sport Media/ Sipa U / SIPA ; **p. 31**-mg1 ph © Amy Myers / Shutterstock ; **p. 31**-mg2 ph © theshots.co / Shutterstock ; **p. 32**-hg ph © Adobe/Ilona Baha; p. 32-mg ph © Brad Loper / Fort Worth Star-Telegram / Tribune News Service via Getty Images ; **p. 32**-md © Adobe/Olena Rublenko ; **p. 33**-hg ph © Adobe/deagreez ; **p. 33**-mh1 ph © Adobe/Hunman ; **p. 33**-mh2 ph © Adobe/comicsans ; **p. 33**-mh3 ph © SUSA / Icon Sport ; **p. 33**-hd ph © Tom Pidgeon / Getty Images North America / Getty Images via AFP; **p. 33**-m1 ph © Wesley Hitt / Getty Images North America / Getty Images via AFP ; **p. 33**-m2 ph © Photo by Steven King / Icon Sportswire via Getty Images; p. **33**-m3 ph © Adobe/New Africa; **p. 35**-m1 ph Shutterstock/AlivePhoto ; **p. 35**-m2 ph Cavan Images / Alamy Stock Photo ; **p.37**-mg1 ph © Adobe/aldorado ; **p. 37**-mg2 ph © Adobe/fifg ; **p. 37**-mg3 ph © Adobe/yan4ik ; **p. 37**-mg4 ph © Adobe/Hunman ; **p. 37**-mg5 ph © Adobe/WawX ; **p. 37**-mg6 ph © Adobe/dnz ; **p. 39**-m ph © Anna Gill ; **p. 39**-b1 ph © Adobe/R-DESIGN ; **p. 39**-b2 ph © Adobe/sharplaninac ; **p. 39**-b3 ph © Adobe/ompong_tom ; **p. 39**-b4 ph © DigitalVision Vectors ; **p. 40**-hd ph © Photo by Kyle Okita / CSM / REX ; **p. 40**-b1 ph © Photo by Hannah Foslien / Getty Images ; **p. 40**-b2 ph © Justin Edmonds / Getty Images ; **p. 41**-h1 ph © Adobe/william87 ; **p. 41**-h2 ph Adobe/coachwood ; **p. 41**-m ph © Photo by Roy K. Miller / Icon Sportswire / Corbis / Icon Sportswire via Getty Images ; **p. 41**-b ph © Photo by Robin Alam / Icon Sportswire via Getty Images ; **p.42**-43 ph © 2022 C.S. Pacat. All Rights Reserved. Used with Permission ; **p. 44-45** ph © avec l'aimable permission de Notting Hill and Ealing High School ; **p. 46**-© avec l'aimable permission de Notting Hill and Ealing High School ; **p. 46**-bd ph © Getty Images / DigitalVision Vectors ; **p. 47**-h ph © avec l'aimable permission de Notting Hill and Ealing High School ; **p. 48** ph © avec l'aimable permission de Notting Hill and Ealing High School ; **p. 49**-1 ph © Heritage Image Partnership Ltd / Alamy Stock Photo; **p. 49**-2 ph © PictureLux / The Hollywood Archive / Alamy Stock Photo; **p. 49**-3 ph © Pierre Mornet / Portrait de George Eliot; **p. 50**-m ph © Owen Smith / Alamy Banque D'Images ; **p. 51**-h © PHOTOSHOT / MAXPPP ; **p. 52**-b ph © ADOBE/rockindaddy; **p. 53**-hd ph © Science History Images / Alamy Stock Photo ; **p. 54**-b1 ph ©Espen Rasmussen / PANOS / REA ; **p. 54**-b2 ph © Action Images / Keith Williams ; **p. 55**-h ph © PictureLux / The Hollywood Archive /Alamy Stock Photo ; **p.55**-m ph© Domaine public, https://commons.wikimedia.org/w/index.php?curid=1367644 ; **p. 56**-hd ph © COLLECTION CHRISTOPHEL © Warner Bros / HEYDAY FILMS ; **p. 56**-b1 ph © Above, a land tortoise; below, a turtle. Etching by Oudet after P.L. Oudart. Wellcome Collection. Public Domain Mark ; **p. 56**-b2 ph © Adobe/doublebubble_rus ; **p. 56**-b3 ph © Adobe/Hein Nouwens ; **p. 57**-h1/2/3/4 ph © COLLECTION CHRISTOPHEL © Warner Bros / HEYDAY FILMS ; **p. 57**-mg ph © Adobe/Olhapankiv ; **p. 57**-b © ADOBE/dinesh ; **p. 58-59** ph © 2022 C.S. Pacat. All Rights Reserved. Used with Permission ; **p. 60-61** ph Collection Christophel © Lionsgate / Mandeville films / Participant media / Walden media ; **p. 62**-hg ph © Birch Path Literary, D.R ; **p. 62**-md ph © Christophel_photo_bf.Wonder_2017_031 ; **p. 62**-b ph © Birch Path Literary, D.R ; **p. 63**-hd ph © Adobe/Matt ; **p. 63**-mg ph © Lifestyle pictures / Alamy Stock Photo ; **p. 63**-md ph © Birch Path Literary, D.R ; **p. 64**-hg ph © Birch Path Literary, D.R ; **p. 64**-hd ph Collection Christophel © Lionsgate / Mandeville films / Participant media / Walden media ; **p. 65**-md ph © Photo: Dale Robinette Credit: Lionsgate / BBQ_DFY / Aurimages ; **p. 66**-m ph © Photo: Dale Robinette Credit: Lionsgate / BBQ_DFY / Aurimages ; **p. 67**-m ph © Tad Carpenter / Penguin Random House LLC ; **p. 69**-h1 ph © Birch Path Literary, D.R ; **p. 69**-h2 ph © Birch Path Literary, D.R ; **p. 70**-md ph © Birch Path Literary, D.R **p. 71**-bg ph © Shutterstock/Chekyravaa ; **p. 72**-md ph © Storyboard That / https://www.storyboardthat.com/ ; **p. 73**-hg ph © Bridgeman / Mark Gerson / By permission of Llyfrgell Genedlaethol Cymru / The National Library of Wales ; **p. 73**-m1 ph © Mr Paul Green, Saint Wilfrid's CofE Academy ; **p. 73**-m2 ph Getty Images © Photo by Brent N. Clarke / FilmMagic Brent ; **p. 73**-bg ph © Birch Path Literary, D.R ; **p. 74-75** ph © 2022 C.S. Pacat. All Rights Reserved. Used with Permission ; **p. 76 à 83**-fond ph © Shutterstock/merrymuuu : **p. 78**-hg ph © antonpix / Shutterstock ; **p. 78**-b ph © Hans Holbein the Younger/Galleria Nazionale d'Arte Antica/Adam Eastland Art + Architecture / Alamy Banque D'Images ; **p. 79**-h1 ph © Adobe/diquesvet ; **p. 79**-h2 ph © Adobe/Yvonne Wawro ; **p.79**-h3 ph © Sodacan, CCBY-SA3.0 ; **p. 79**-h4 ph © ADOBE/ ug; **p. 79**-h5 ph © Sodacan, CCBY-SA3.0 ; **p. 79**-h6 ph © Adobe/Yul ; **p. 79**-b ph © Stefano Bianchetti / Bridgeman Images ; **p. 80-81** Copyright © Historic Royal Palaces 2022, D.R ; **p. 80**-b ph © Shutterstock/Epitavi ; **p. 83**-b ph © Hans Holbein the Younger/Galleria Nazionale d'Arte Antica/Adam Eastland Art + Architecture / Alamy Banque D'Images ; **p. 84-85** ph © 2022 C.S. Pacat. All Rights Reserved. Used with Permission ; **p. 86-87** ph © Heather Leah Kennedy ; **p. 88**-1 ph COLLECTION CHRISTOPHEL © Netflix - Entertainment 360 - Grey Matters Productions; **p. 88**-2 ph COLLECTION CHRISTOPHEL © Warner Bros. - Heyday Films ; **p. 88**-3 ph © Warner Bros / EVERETT / Aurimages ; **p. 89**-hd ph © Alamo Drafthouse Cinema, LLC ; **p. 89**-mg ph © Danjaq / MGM / BBQ_DFY / Aurimages ; **p. 89**-m ph © Adobe/Tartila ; **p. 90**-h1 ph © brando, FLICKR (CC BY 2.0) ; **p. 90**-h2 ph © Heather Leah Kennedy ; **p. 90**-h3 ph © Adobe/New Africa ; **p. 90**-mg1 ph © Heather Leah Kennedy ; **p. 90**-mg2 ph © Adobe/shersor ; **p. 90**-mg3 ph © Adobe/Gresei ; **p. 90**-mg4 ph © Adobe/ba baz ; **p. 90**-bg ph © Michael Neelon(misc) / Alamy Stock Photo ; **p. 90-91**-m ph © Alamo Drafthouse Cinema, LLC ; **p. 92**-m1 ph © Adobe/ Gelpi ; **p.92**-m2 ph © Fuse / Corbis / Getty ; **p. 92**-bd ph © Adobe/Tartila ; **p. 95**-h1 ph Warner Bros / BBQ_DFY / Aurimages ; **p. 95**-h2 ph ©Universal Pictures / Courtesy Everett Collection / Aurimages ; **p. 95**-h3 ph Walt Disney Pictures / BBQ_DFY / Aurimages ; **p. 95**-mg ph © Adobe/kazy ; **p. 95**-bd ph © Adobe/David ; **p. 96**-1 ph © Adobe/Joe ; **p. 96**-2 ph © dpa picture qalliance / Alamy Stock Photo ; **p. 96**-3 ph © Adobe/Konstantin Zibert ; **p. 96**-4 ph © Adobe/serhiibobyk ; **p. 97**-m1 ph © Adobe/azurita ; **p. 97**-m2 ph © Adobe/azurita ; **p. 98**-1 ph © By Cla1402group4 - Own work, CC BY-SA 4.0, https://commons.wikimedia.org/w/index.php?curid=47719234 ; **p. 98**-2 ph © Mindspace / iStock by Getty Images ; **p. 98**-3 ph © Adobe/kkavve ; **p. 98-99**-mb ph © J R Eyerman / The LIFE Picture Collection / Shutterstock ; **p. 99**-b ph © Joe Raedle / Getty Images / AFP ; **p. 99**-md1 ph © Heather Leah Kennedy ; **p. 99**-md2 ph © Alamo Drafthouse Cinema, LLC ; **p. 100-101** ph © 2022 C.S. Pacat. All Rights Reserved. Used with Permission ; **p. 102-103** ph © picture alliance / imageBROKER | Valentin Wolf ; **p. 104**-hg ph © Adobe/eldadcarin ; **p. 104**-m ph © Prod DB © Sony - Columbia Pictures - Marvel Entertainment / DR ; **p. 105**-m1 ph © Adobe/Helena Garcia ; **p. 105**-m2 ph © Adobe/dell ; **p. 106**-hg ph © Adobe/ eldadcarin ; **p. 107**-hd1 ph © Adobe/Pineapple studio ; **p. 107**-hd2 ph © Adobe/Ljupco Smokovski ; **p. 106**-m1 ph © By Vector adopted by User:NafsadhOriginal:Julius Schorzman, Public Domain, https://commons.wikimedia.org/w/index.php?curid=36401671; **p. 106**-m3 ph © Lycée Français de New York, D.R ; **p. 107**-hd1 ph **p. 111**-h1 ph © Adobe/Mariana Ianovska ; **p. 111**-h2 ph © Adobe/Luciano Mortula-LGM ; **p. 112**-b1 ph © Adobe/valeriyap ; **p. 112**-b2 ph © KK Stock / Shutterstock ; **p. 112**-b3 ph © Patti McConville / Alamy Banque D'Images ; **p. 112**-b4 ph © ShutterstocK/lcdpstock ; **p. 113**-b ph © Adobe/ pjirawat ; **p. 115**-mg ph © Adobe/Arild ; **p. 115**-md ph © Alexander Alland, Jr. / Getty Images ; **p. 115**-bd ph © Betka82/Getty Images ; p. **116-117** ph © 2022 C.S. Pacat. All Rights Reserved. Used with Permission ; **p. 118-119** ph © ferrantraite / Getty Images ; **p. 120**-hg ph © Adobe/Ruslan Gilmanshin ; **p. 120**-1 ph © Steven Gerner / CC BY-SA 2.0 ; **p. 120**-2 ph © Adobe/IndiaPix ; **p. 120**-3 ph © Photo by Dinesh Gupta / Pacific Press ; **p. 121**-d1 ph © Amit Dave / Reuters ; **p. 121**-d2 ph © Adobe/sorayuth26 ; **p. 121**-d3 ph © Adobe/avijit ; **p. 121**-d4 ph © Adobe/cdkproductions; **p. 121**-d5 ph © Adobe/Maksim Kostenkom; **p. 122**-hg ph © Adobe/Ruslan Gilmanshin ; **p. 122**-m1 ph COLLECTION CHRISTOPHEL © Cape of Good Films / Colour Yellow Productions ; **p. 122**-m2 ph © Akash Vukoti ; **p. 123**-h ph © Adobe/phive2015 ; **p. 123**-m ph © Adobe/ bharatmanoj ; **p. 124**-m ph © Luba V Nel / Shutterstock ; **p. 124**-m © Kids World Travel Guide, D.R : **p. 124**-bd ph © Adobe/Arundhati ; **p. 125**-mg ph © Adobe/StockImageFactory ; **p. 125**-md ph © Adobe/Maksim Kostenko ; **p. 127**-h1 ph © Adobe/bharatmanoj ; **p. 127**-h2 ph © Adobe/avijit ; **p. 127**-h3 ph © Adobe/Ruslan Gilmanshin ; **p. 127**-h4 ph © Adobe/Maksim Kostenko ; **p. 128**-md ph © The Learning Curve; D.R ; **p. 130**-h ph © Adobe/StockImageFactory ; **p. 130**-m1 ph © Shruti Ghatak ; **p. 130**-m2 ph © Shruti Ghatak ; **p. 130**-m3 ph © Shruti Ghatak ; **p. 130**-b1 ph © Adobe/Bart ; **p. 130**-b2 ph © Adobe/sanirimpan ; **p. 130**-b3 ph © Adobe/Brent Hofacker ; **p. 130**-b4 ph © Adobe/asab974 ; **p. 131**-h1 ph © Art Directors & TRIP / Alamy Banque D'Images ; **p. 131**-h2 ph © Adobe/sorayuth26 ; **p. 131**-h3 ph © Adobe/jack_sparrow ; **p. 131**-bg ph © Mike Kemp / Getty Images ; **p. 131**-bd ph © ADOBE/ ali saadat/EyeEm ; **p. 132-133** ph © 2022 C.S. Pacat. All Rights Reserved. Used with Permission ; **p. 134-135** ph © Getty Images / wundervisuals ; **p. 136**-hg ph © Adobe/nerthuz ; **p. 136-137**-m ph © Ryan Trahey / Adirondack Camp ; **p. 136**-mg ph © Ryan Trahey / Adirondack Camp ; **p. 137**-h ph © Ryan Trahey / Adirondack Camp ; **p. 137**-m ph © Ryan Trahey / Adirondack Camp ; **p. 138**-hg ph © Adobe/nerthuz ; **p. 138**-mg ph © Copyright 2018, Steven K. Smith ; **p. 140**-bd ph © Adobe/Juriah Mosin ; **p. 143**-md ph © Adobe/nerthuz ; **p. 144**-m1 ph © Adobe/chekman ; **p. 144**-m2 ph © Adobe/SVIATOSLAV ; **p. 145**-m1 ph © Adobe/Sergi ; **p. 145**-m2 ph © Monkey Business Images / Shutterstock ; **p. 145**-m3 ph © Adobe/Peter Atkins ; **p. 145**-m4 ph © Adobe/Nick ALDI ; **p. 146**-hd ph © Adobe/dusk ; **p. 146**-bd ph © PeopleImages / Getty Images ; **p. 148-149** ph © 2022 C.S. Pacat. All Rights Reserved. Used with Permission ; **p. 153** ph © Striking Images - Tourism Ireland / Alamy Stock Photo ; **p. 154**-hd ph © iStock / Getty Images Plus ; **p. 154**-bg ph © Photo by Clodagh Kilcoyne / Getty Images ; **p. 154**-bm © Szymon Barylski / Alamy Stock Photo ; **p. 154**-bd © Bonzo / Alamy Live News ; **p. 155**-m1 ph © Richard Milnes / Alamy Live New ; **p. 155**-m2 ph © Paul Brown / Alamy Stock Photo ; **p. 155**-m3 ph © Simeon 69 / Shutterstock ; **p. 155**-m4 ph © Zoonar GmbH / Alamy Stock Photo ; **p. 156**-hd ph © Adobe/mykolastock ; **p. 156**-mg ph © George Sweeney / Alamy Live News ; **p. 156**-md ph © Striking Images - Tourism Ireland / Alamy Stock Photo ; **p. 156** mb ph © ADOBE/ nixki ; **p. 156**-bd ph © Adobe/Africa Studio

DR : Malgré nos efforts, il nous a été impossible de joindre certains auteurs ou leurs ayants-droit pour solliciter l'autorisation de reproduction, nous avons réservé en notre comptabilité les droits usuels

Achevé d'imprimer en France par Pollina - 13556 – Dépôt légal : 10512-0/01 - Avril 2022

IMPRIM'VERT®

The English-speaking world

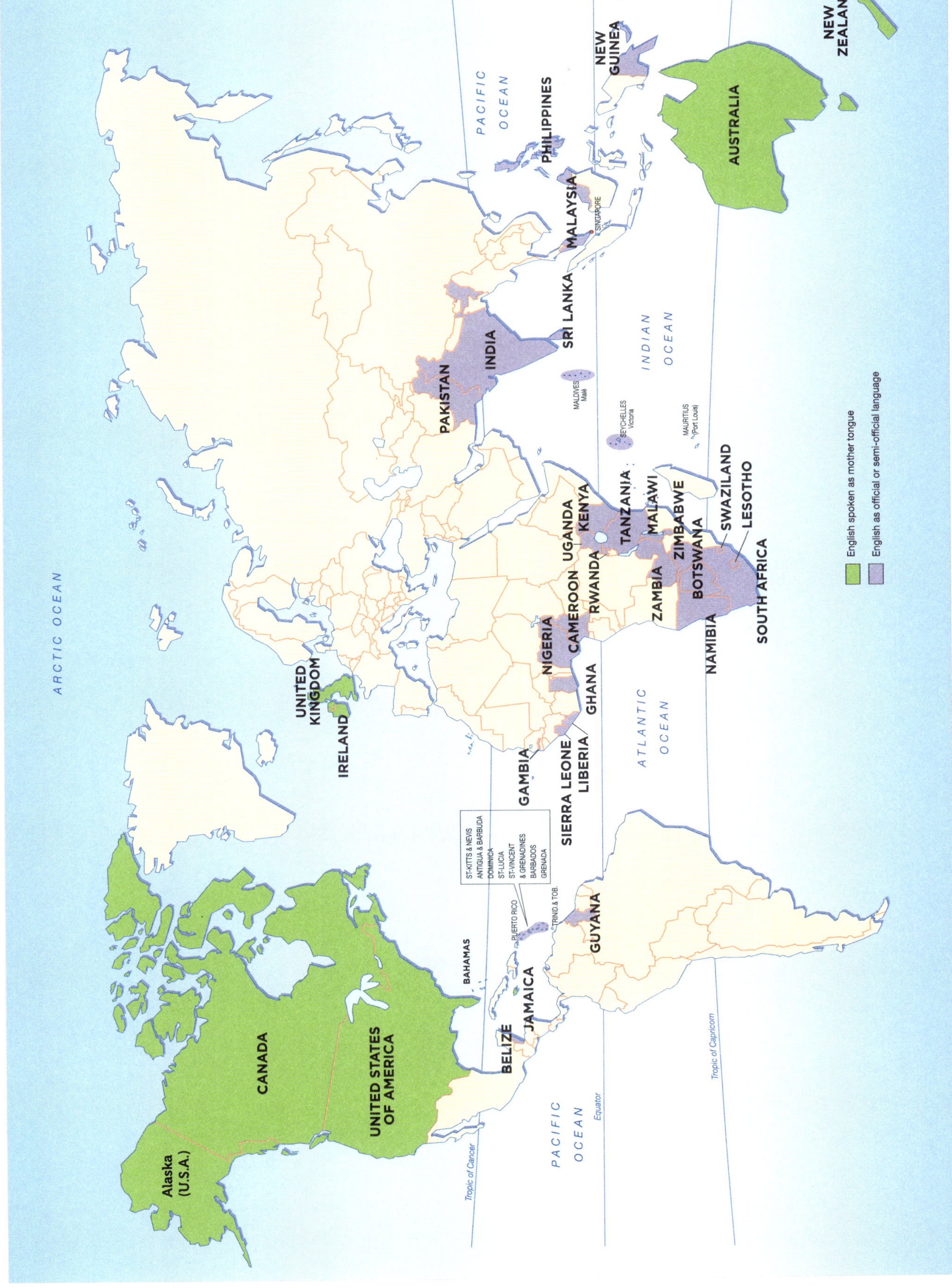

The British Isles